W9-CLE-737

Maximized Relationship

"Creating The Rhythm

In Your Relationship"

A Self Help Guide to a Healthy Relationship

By

Donna Ritchie

Donna Ritchie

Unless otherwise indicated, all Scripture quotations are taken from the King James Version Life Application Bible. Copywritten 1986, 1988, 1989 by Tyndale House Publishers, Inc., Wheaton Illinois 60189.

Maximized Relationship

Creating the Rhythm in Your Relationship.

A Self Help Guide to a Healthy Relationship

By: Donna Ritchie

ISBN-13: 978-1502590749

ISBN-10: 1502590743

Published By: It's All About Him Media & Publishing

A Multimedia Division of

True Love Church of Refuge

5201-D Nations Ford Road, Charlotte, NC 28217

Aahmp.weebly.com

980-522-8096

Edited by Delisa Lindsey

Copyright © 2004 by Donna Ritchie

Web: www.donnaritchie.com

Cover Design: Delisa Lindsey

Printed in the United States of America.

All rights reserved under International Copyright Law.

Contents and/or cover may not be reproduced in whole or in part in any form without the express written consent of the Publisher.

Foreword

This book you hold in your hand is designed to challenge your perception as it pertains to relationships. It is a learning process for those who are married and those contemplating marriage. It is not gender specific. Life's challenges does not discriminate; it affects both male and female.

If you desire to grow up and receive the maximum potential in your relationship, this book is for you. You will never be the same after reading this book. It will revolutionize your thinking. Sometimes it is difficult to see ourselves when the spotlight is on us, however a wise person listens and adheres to instruction.

With God first in your life no one else is more important than your spouse. Since God instituted marriage, it is only fair to consult Him for the intricate details of that union. You will be amazed at what He says about married life and its details. You will be astounded at the ideas He will equip you with to maintain a healthy and harmony filled life with the one you love. However, it starts with you. This book is designed for YOU.

I am persuaded that you will greatly benefit from the principles in this book. My intent is to see you and your spouse living in a happy, loving, excited, and healthy relationship.

Donna Ritchie

Table Of Contents

Donna Ritchie

About The Author

Donna Ritchie is a native of Detroit, Michigan who was partially raised in Montgomery, Alabama. She is highly respected by her peers as a gifted Musician, Producer, and Recording Artist. She stems from a Christian background with much thanks to her parents, Bishop Donald Ritchie and the late Mrs. Lucille Ritchie of Montgomery, Alabama. She has six brothers and two sisters.

Donna is happily married to the love of her life, Leon Johnson, and they have a beautiful daughter named Diamond.

Donna Ritchie has traveled the world and connected with millions for nearly two decades as a Multi-Award Winning International Television Host and Inspirational Singer. She is one of three Co-hosts of the popular Daytime TV Show Series, *Friends and Neighbors*, which has entered almost two decades of production on stations across the world with each episode carrying the theme of enriching lives physically, emotionally, and spiritually. Having been highly recognized in Hollywood, California for Excellence in Christian Media and with worldwide acclaim, *Friends and Neighbors* has showcased such topics as the world of Entertainment, The American Heart Association, The School Of Culinary Arts, charitable organizations, various authors, entrepreneurs, relationship guidance, health and fitness and has also featured her singing a ballad from her latest release. Donna is proud to note that *Friends and Neighbors* was honored with a Silver Angel Award for Excellence in Christian Media from Hollywood, California, a Telly Award, which receives over 11,000 entries from all 50 states and 5 continents and honors the very best local, regional, and cable television commercials and programs. It has also received the finest video and film productions and work created for the Web and a Gabby Award from the Georgia Association of Broadcasters. These productions were recognized and rewarded for their professional approach and having the highest "moral, ethical and social impact" with the focus on, "Together we are making a better world with programming for families and children of all ages!" She has also hosted the popular nightly show, *Atlanta LIVE*.

As an Emmy Nominated Singer who has gained the accolades and respect of her peers, Donna is one of Contemporary Christian Music's most compelling singers. Her style of singing has always been intensely her own and has inspired millions. She compassionately interacts with her audience and takes them to the ultimate musical level. She confidently charges and sets the atmosphere.

Donna's expertise on relational rhythm comes from her very own personal experience and living through others stories and comments. It takes a wise person to conclude that if something works or doesn't work one must adapt and adjust especially in relationship. Since God instituted marriage, His word is the manual by which we reference relationship. Refer to Him often and you will be surprised at how "Down To Earth" He really is.

Acknowledgements

I would like to thank my wonderful husband, Leon, for your love and support, spoken and unspoken. I have learned a lot from you as a man, as my husband, and father of my child. There are so many good things in you that I aspire to become. Yes! You are the king in our castle and being your queen is my all time pleasure. Loving you is so easy to do. Thank you for that.

To my loving, kind daughter, Diamond, who is a special gift given to us from Heaven. Diamond, thank you for being a beautiful daughter, inside and out. When I think of the words, happy, compassionate, smart, gifted, sweet, and loveable, I think of you. I love you beyond words.

Thank you to my parents, Bishop Donald Ritchie and the late Mrs. Lucille Ritchie for my upbringing and instilling in me wisdom and God's way of dealing with life and all it has to offer. Thank you for being a stable and firm foundation for me to build my life upon. You are the best parents a girl could ever wish for. Thank you for being the mother and father of all of my siblings whom I love to the core. Thanks to all six of my brothers and two sisters for being a part of my existence.

I want to thank my publisher, Delisa Lindsey, of "It's All About Him" Media and Publishing. Thank you for stepping in at the right time. Your timing and expertise stands tall in the remarkable section. Thank you for your added touch.

I want to dedicate this book to my family and all those who are in a relationship and are trying to make it work. Anything in life that is worth something takes work but the bottom line is that its outcome consequently yields rewarding benefits.

Maximized Relationship

1

Yours For The Asking

I would like to pose the question to you. What kind of mate are you seeking? What kind of relationship are you looking for? What do you have to bring to the table of a relationship or to someone else's life? Is what you are asking for a reality or fiction?

It is amazing the countless perception people have concerning what they are looking for in a mate or in a relationship. There are those who say, " I want someone who's going to make me happy." I agree you deserve to be happy but who better to make you happiest than you? No  one can ever make you as happy as you can make yourself. What an awesome task to place on someone else when happiness lies within.

You have everything you need inside of you to make you happy. A mate should add to what is already there. There should be a happiness in you that satisfies you to your ultimate satisfaction and to bring someone else into your life is to add to what is already exuberantly there.

Some say, " I want someone who is going to satisfy me". Here again, no one can satisfy you like you can satisfy yourself. God never designed a human being who can totally satisfy you. They can satisfy you for a while but the long lasting, deep satisfaction you're looking for only comes from God. Then there's that part of satisfaction that only you can do for yourself. You must be satisfied with yourself, first and foremost. It is so unfair to make a person feel the need to satisfy YOU totally. Look, if you can't do it for yourself, no one, I repeat, no one else can do it for you either.

A mate can only add to what is already there. What if your mate was looking for that in you? Can you deliver such an awesome request? If you can, then by all means do so. What I am trying to do is prompt you to carefully think about what you really want, whether it is in a relationship or in life. You can have what you desire but consider the whole picture. When it involves someone else you must take into consideration his or her ideas, opinions, and desires. No one aspires to be in a relationship where they will have to spend all their time working on you, toiling, laboring, and wrestling with you and for you, and having to suffer with those habits that will really damper those around you. Good relationships come with the idea of one wanting to spend the rest of their life with you because they love you and they feel comfortable with you. They feel you are an asset to their life. You are a positive enhancement for their life.

If you are happy and satisfied with yourself then a mate only magnifies that. Oh, and here's a good one, "I want to marry a rich man or woman". Perhaps you have not considered what a rich mate prefers in their mate? Have you considered what you are asking for in a mate? Do you know how to budget? Do you know how to keep a leveled head when you walk into a rich lifestyle? Do you know how to run a business? Do you know how to take care of business? There are those who might say, "I want to marry someone who is independent". Someone who is independent comes with certain mindsets and ways of doing various tasks as independent people do. Independent people can make you feel like they can live life without you. Why? Because they are independent people. You have to be strong and confident enough in yourself to know how to really understand an independent person, their needs, and how they operate. My question to you is, "Are you really prepared to handle an independent person?"

Maybe you are looking for that Mr. Universe or Miss America and they have not considered what Mr. Universe or Miss America wants in their mate. I'm sure they'd love to have someone who is physically fit; someone with gorgeous features both inside and out. What I am saying is when you are looking for certain qualities in a mate, first take a good look at yourself and honestly ask yourself, "What can I bring to a relationship?" "How can I enhance his or her life?" Find out what that person you are seeking for is like, and generally what they are seeking for in a relationship. Knowledge is power. In all of your getting, get understanding. Understanding a thing will take you a long way in life for the better.

I remember during my single days writing down certain qualities I wanted in a man and asking God for them. I also remember saying to myself, "Whomever this man is, I am going to love him". I immediately began thinking of ways I was planning to enhance his life and ways I wanted to make him happy, not how I can manipulate him to be what I wanted him to be or how I can change him. No one likes to be changed in that aspect. Everyone loves to be himself or herself and it is utterly difficult and frustrating to have to be forced to change.

Just think about 'how would you like it if someone forced you to change to be something you are not?' Just the thought of that leaves a bad taste in your mouth. It is much easier to be yourself.

Accepting someone for who they are makes it easy for them to love you more. Think about it. When you meet your significant other, namely the one you are going to marry, you decide you want to get married and the two of you become engaged looking forward to marriage. What you are saying 'Yes' to in the proposal is, "I accept you for who are." You are saying, "Yes", to the, "As Is", right? As puzzling as it seems, there are those who are single and successful in life, male and/or female with the opposite sex screaming and yelling for their attention.

Let's take a closer look at what you are seeking in a mate. For example, you have a successful, single male who decides to settle down with this girl. At first, she really liked what she saw but did not want to let on that she was diggin' him and was screaming, trying to get his attention. She was attracted to his successful life-style; his looks, his notoriety, and his money. Once she gets his attention and he wants to date and then marry her, she has a kid (purely out of love or sometimes for collateral), then she complains because he has no time for her and the kids. Think about it for a second realistically. He was busy when you met him and when he proposed and she said, "Yes", she said 'Yes' to his schedule and his lifestyle. Now please understand this is not everyone who is successful. This is just an example. Let's be real about it because this does happen although I do not know anyone personally in this situation. Needless to say, she marries into a busy, hectic lifestyle. Yeah, I know you're probably thinking, "Well he was not too busy. He noticed me." True. But then over time, she decides she can't take his lifestyle anymore. It's too much for her. Granted he still loves her; he's faithful. He provides for her and takes good care of his family but she still wants a separation and possibly a divorce just because she cannot deal with his lifestyle. What I am saying is before making a decision like this that will affect him, your children, and yes, yourself, think about it. This is what you said 'Yes' to.

Relationships are a two way street. Before making a life changing decision to get married, please step back and carefully count up the cost. Are you willing and able to live with this kind of life? Do you understand his definition of, "I love you?" Do you understand what she is really looking for in your relationship? We will talk about understanding your man and understanding your woman later on in this book. We will discover what men and women perceive as love and life.

When in doubt always, always, always ASK questions. What you don't know can hurt you. The Bible tells us, "With all your getting, get an understanding". Getting an understanding literally means, 'the ability to comprehend and judge; to be intelligent about something; to get a mutual agreement.' You want to do this BEFORE getting married in every aspect of the word. Careful observation in dating is very critical. Observing the spoken and the unspoken behavior is necessary.

When you are contemplating marriage it is imperative to know as much as possible because in marriage you are sharing your life with someone else and vice versa. You open yourself to become vulnerable in marriage and you want to know the strength of your foundation before the building process goes underway. I am not saying to be on the defensive guard but watch and observe. Sometimes to be over defensive, you will lose the thing you desire; often times a good thing, however to become passive you sometimes forfeit your happiness in return. There are many spoken and unspoken words, gestures, gleams, and expressions that are silent assurances. A wise man or woman will learn to see it, hear it, and understand it. Ladies, when you discover it, you will realize whether or not you have found Mr. Right or for the men, you will know if you have found a good thing in your lady friend. You will both discover whether you were really meant to be together, if you are truly soul mates, or if your relationship should remain on a friendly basis. You will know if you were destined for each other. It is so exciting when you find it! When considering marriage, it is imperative that the both of you expect it to work and work it. So keep reading my friend because Knowledge IS Power!

2

Seek and You Will Find

When you are seeking a mate to spend the rest of your life with, you will want to consider someone who is interested in the same things you are interested in. Having something in common is a good thing. The more the merrier. For an example, you love to play tennis and it is a high priority on your list of hobbies, you might want to find someone who likes tennis, someone who likes physical exercise, or you want to find someone who supports you playing tennis. Finding someone who is a good team player in life is a great and wonderful thing. If you think about it, good relationships are made of people who are team players. Team players are adaptable, they will take care of their load, and are willing to help you especially when there is a need. Team players are goal oriented, they just want to get the overall job done. But keep in mind team players need team players in order for them to become most effective.

What I am saying is whatever your preference, find out what kind of person they are; what kind of mindset do they have. Do your homework and find out as much as you can about your preference. Whomever you choose for a mate find out what you have in common. If what you have in common is high on your list of priorities, that is a plus for your relationship. However, keep in mind that when in doubt about anything and everything please ask questions. What you are doing is building an effective line of communication and getting an understanding before you commit to a long lasting relationship. Get to know one another and do not get so caught up in the bliss of being in love that you lose your sight. Pay attention to one another and if you have begun a relationship, be attentive to the climate of your relationship. What do I mean by climate? The atmosphere and how that person makes you feel when they are around. How do you feel about yourself when you are with them. These are things you want to keep in mind and communicate throughout the relationship because it will be very helpful if you decide to settle in and marry. We will talk about understanding and communicating later on in the book.

Understanding one another is essential in communicating

3

Initial Approach

There is the saying, "Image is everything", and that is true. The correct approach and presentation is everything too! The way you approach a person determines their response to you. An approach consists of the words used, the tone of voice, body language. A relationship's approach consists of the other person's perception of you or their misconception of you. How do you approach your mate concerning various subjects?

Often times in many marital relationships the respect over time tends to get lost in the shuffle of life and taking one another for granted subtly creeps in. We get so comfortable and loose that we say and do anything. This is the beginning of marital breakdown. When you get loose in your relationship you start the process of disrespect, thus the relationship starts to head downward. I hear many people say, "I want him or her to be this or that", but what are you doing to make it happen? In a marital relationship you can make or break your mate. You can enhance and better your relationship or you can tear it down and slice your own hand. Some people are so mean that it brings out the beast in their mate! I have met people who say, "You know I want a Christian mate", and they live like somebody paid them to be a devil themselves. Now tell me what can you do for a Christian mate? Would you enhance their Christianity or make them a devil by your actions? Would you tear them down or make them become what you are expecting them to be? Look, if you want a Christian mate, if you want the perfect person, of whom there are none, it is only wise you become what you want others to be first. This is where the statement references, "When you walk in my shoes for a while, then I can listen to you; then we can talk". Relationships are not designed to make someone miserable but are designed to enhance someone else.

Marital relationships are designed for two people to love one another as Christ loves the church. I have never heard Christ beat the church, slander the church, or make the church miserable. He loves the church unconditionally. Are you treating your mate like Christ treats the church? Often times we place high levels of expectancy on our mate while making excuses and allowances for what is expectant of ourselves. What am I saying? Here's what I am saying, the thing we expect from our spouse is the very thing we neglect to do ourselves or we do it to prove a point and not because we need to do it regardless. This kind of behavior and mindset is so unfair. Whatever you expect from others you must always be willing to first be a partaker of it yourself or a participant and if your mate is not meeting your level of expectancy, then leave it to God and accept whatever the outcome maybe. There are countless times when you leave a situation alone, stop worrying about it, and cast that care on God that it may change for the better or you will eventually overcome it and the outcome renders a peaceable resolution. If you are what you expect in others then ask God to give you peace and be willing to accept the outcome. What I mean by accept the outcome is this. Sometimes the outcome will not be what you expected. Can you live with that? Sometimes, time itself will change it or it may not change. Sensibly ask yourself is it worth giving up the good times? Is it worth giving up on your relationship?

Marital relationships are not designed to see how much one can change the other but accepting and loving the other person 'AS IS.' Have you heard someone say to their child or have you ever said to your child, "You're just like your Mother", or, "You're just like your Father", with disgust in their voice? Well has it ever dawned on you that you chose their Mom or Dad? See, we must be careful of what we say. Your children are a gift from God and you have a responsibility to train them up in the way of God. When you speak negative over them or anyone for that matter, you are molding them. Speak positive words over your children and over your spouse. Matt 12:36 says, "We are going to give an account to God for every word we say." What I am trying to emphasize is, in this world of, "If it feels good, do it", you cannot just say or do anything to your mate or to others. The Bible speaks about self-control and discipline so many times. We must get this in our spirit. We live in a society that is infused in anger. It takes nothing for one to get angry these days.

One of the reasons there are so many divorces today is that people just give up fighting. We are so engulfed in life itself that we give up fighting for what is most important in our lives. Your marital relationship is worth fighting for. Everyone is looking for love but divorces are at an all time high. What's up with that? That is so contradictory. We make decisions on top of decisions and sometimes we are clueless of the effects it has on others and us. A bad decision causes health risks.

I remember as a child we used to say, "Sticks and Stones may break my bones but words will never hurt me." Oh, but how untrue. Words are the things you can never retrieve. You may say, "I'm Sorry", but the words are still out there. Your words are so powerful (good or bad). Even God thinks your words are powerful. Your words are so powerful that He says He will judge us by every word that comes out of our mouths. Your words have life and death in them. They are powerful. That is why one of the first things God literally spoke to me when I got married concerning my spouse was about my words. I cannot just say anything to him. I must be careful of how I speak to him and my tone. Why? Out of respect, which is something everyone deserves and as time goes on in relationship, deeply earns. Why? Because he belongs to God. God made him. He has a soul too. Your spouse is human and has feelings. Always respect them. Respect them in your words and your behavior. And respect them all the more, if respect is what you expect in return. "Do unto others as you would have them do unto you."

Take time to enjoy something you both like together

4

Making the Right Choice

I want to prompt you to seriously think about the choices you make. Your choices affect you and those around you, especially those closest to you. Think about it. When you were dating and your present spouse asked you to marry them and you said, "Yes!!", with tears in your eyes and your heart beating so fast you could not keep up with it. Did it ever dawn on you to ask, "Who am I marrying?" And for the one whose asking your hand in marriage, be it male or female, have you ever stopped to think, "What kind of world am I asking this person to be a part of?"

When you ask someone to marry you, you are asking him or her into your life. You are inviting them into your world and you are asking them into the secret areas of your life too. My question to you is this. What kind of life are you proposing to them? What kind of world are you inviting them to become a part of? Are you prepared to enhance their life? To add to their life? What are you bringing to the table? To those that say ecstatically, "Yes, I will marry you", do you know what "Yes" means? Yes means, Yes. I want to be a part of your life, your world. Yes, I love you as you are! Yes, means I want to and I am willing to work at making our relationship better, stronger, and long lasting. Yes, I want to work with you in making our marriage work. Sadly enough I hear parents tell their kids in utter disgust, "You know you are just like your Daddy", or "You got those bad habits from your Mother."

The child, feeling bad enough, feels worse and torn because the ones he or she loves most (Mom and Dad), are now criticizing them. Consequently, this statement rips a hole right in their heart which sometimes backfires on you, the accuser. It shakes their foundation in life.

The Bible talks about us being as little children. Children see the good in their parents despite what the parents think of one another. That is why divorce is very difficult on children. Divorce tears them apart emotionally; foundationally. Parents, you are your children's lease in life. Parents are the first and most influential adults in a child's life. The way children interact with adults is a reflection of their interaction with their own parents. Parents, husbands, and wives need to see and focus on the good in each other and highlight it all the time. Parents must stop bad mouthing each other. No one wants his or her faults highlighted. Most times one knows his/her faults and shortcomings without a word being spoken. Also the devil highlights them enough and taunts us to utter frustration at times.

Because you or your spouse did not get along does not mean your children or anyone else for that matter should be included in your disagreement. Believe it or not, you are your children's foundation in life. Because they love you so unconditionally, they want to know, even though you may disagree, that you still love each other even if not the same as before. They need to know that you will always have a place in your heart for them. You spent a part of your life with them. You may have children with them. Every child would like to know they were conceived out of love and not hate. Sometimes reality to a child is too much for them to handle or grasp. That's why God gave them parents.

You wonder why your child misbehaves or is temperamental. It might be because children do what they see. Children are keen to atmospheres, climates, and environments. If you have been arguing, when a child walks in the room, he or she senses it. It is not a good feeling. It is nerve wrecking. It shakes their foundation in life, is a frightful reality, and scares and scars them. So, your words, which is another chapter too, must be tempered. What you do not realize is your baby's daddy or mama was your choice!

You do know that marriage is a work in progress. Unfortunately, good and bad marriage takes work! A good marriage is work coupled with lots of understanding, observation, communication, give and take, and patience, just to name a few. A bad marriage takes bitter effort. Do you know how much better your marriage or relationship would be if you didn't argue so much? Do you know how good your marriage would be if you focused on the good things about your relationship and about your mate? Do you know how wonderful your marriage would be if the two of you worked as a team complimenting one another? Do you know how improved you would be, your health would be, your children would be, and your spouse would be if you mentally focused on the positive things in life in your relationship with others? As you mentally focus on the good thing you have in one another, your language will change for the better, your attitude will change, your behavior will even change.

I love you for who you are.

5

The Art Of a Good Relationship

Good relationships do exist. First of all, since God ordained marriage and manufactured it, it is only wise to consult the Creator, the Originator, and the Manufacturer through prayer and through His word. When your car breaks down, you consult the dealer or the manual for repairs. Well, we should do the same when it comes to marriage. You will be surprised at how down to earth God is. You will be surprised at His response to your relationship. He really does speak to you, your spirit, that inner voice deep down within your belly. Ironically enough, He shines the light on you first because He cares for both of you. He will not tell you to do something that will harm the other. Why? He cares for the both of you. So He shines the light on you and instructs you first. Whether you honestly listen and do it, is up to you. If you don't recognize His voice, ask Him again and He will speak to you again. Sometimes when there is a crisis in marriage we consult the therapist or the psychiatrist but the problem continues to exist. Since the marriage typically started at the altar, we should take it back to the altar and consult the One who ordained it. Everything God makes is beautiful. Marriage is beautiful when you go by His instructions.

A good marriage means understanding your mate. Get to know their heart. Observe what your spouse is really like, especially when they don't think you are noticing them. Find out what makes him or her tick. Find out and understand why they do what they do. Find out so you can bring out their best. Find out so you can be their best friend and partner. The Bible refers to marriage as 'two becoming one'. I looked up the word *become* or *becoming* and it means, "To *come or grow to be, to suit; to be right for; suitable to the wearer.*" If you will notice it does not say, *to arrive.* It does not elude that you have made it.

'Two becoming one' means you will always *be coming* until death do you part. I like to say you will be, 'ever learning', which is what makes the world go around. That seems like a long time but guess what? That is what makes marriage interesting, fun, and intriguing. If you learned all there is to know about marriage and your spouse, can you guess how boring life would be after that? Life is a lesson to learn until death.

A good marriage is 'not jumping to the wrong conclusions'. Sometimes in relationships we destroy the thing we hold dear by jumping to the wrong conclusion. The Bible says, "Be swift, quick, to hear and slow to speak". Why do you think it says that? Because God knew you would speak about things you do not know of. He knew you would speak words that will damage your mate, the one He loves too. However, you will be amazed at what you learn when you follow this rule. Sometimes it is not what you think. Be willing to listen, not just hear, but actually listen attentively.

A good marriage takes prayer. I used to hear the saying, "A family that prays together, stays together". Well that goes for a marriage too. I know you think this is corny and useless, but it works. You will not feel a lightning bolt strike you and thunder will not roll, but you will discover over time, it works. There should not be a day pass that you and your spouse should not pray together. If it's nothing but, "Hello Jesus! How are you? Keep us married and help us to be the best husband or wife to our mate". And yes, call their name. Just as you prayed and asked God for a mate, you must pray and ask God to help you and your mate stay together and stay strong.

Ask God to help you be a better husband or wife to your mate. You should love your spouse so much so that you want to be a better person for them. Now I'm talking about your relationship with your mate, not your relationship with yourself. If you do not have yourself together, you cannot be an asset to your mate. That will not happen. That's another chapter. We are talking about your relationship with your spouse. A good marriage is tempered with kind words, expressions of love, and positive accolades. A good relationship cherishes the other, never takes the other for granted.

In a good marriage, the words:

Thank you,

Excuse me,

I'm sorry,

Forgive me,

Hello or Good Morning, How are you?,

Have a great day?,

How was your day?,

Good night!,

How would you like your eggs cooked?,

I love you; you want to know why?,

You look good, and

I just called because I was thinking about you, are all must haves. These words, rightly spoken, should always be used every day. It keeps the climate between the two of you refreshed, clean, and habitable. I challenge you to start using these words and phrases and observe how the climate changes. Will it happen overnight? Maybe it will, maybe it will not but in time it will change for the better. The Bible talks about overcoming evil with good. Every marriage has great potential. The commitment and teamwork defines a good, thriving, positive relationship. Effortlessness, negativity, and a pessimistic disposition inevitably forms a difficult relationship filled with tumultuous challenges. It is not that a good marriage and a good relationship does not incur rough terrain, it just means with commitment and teamwork, the good potential will prevail and in turn the evil that could prevail is overcome with good. Which one will you and your spouse choose?

Having a good, working relationship must be a choice between the two of you. It is like having Christ work in your life versus having Him not work in your life. Having Him working in your life makes it easier. It is not that you will not have any challenges, it is just that with Him, He makes dealing with life's challenges less difficult. If you do not have Him working in your life then when life's challenges comes knocking at your door, you are defenseless. God gives you wisdom and common sense, in dealing with life's challenges. You will be amazed at how down to earth God is. He is concerned about the details of your life. He wants you to prosper in your relationships, in your business, your finances, and in all aspects of your life.

When you see two people happy, it is not because they do not have problems. It is that they have made the choice of working together to iron out their differences. It is crucial to change your outlook on life. Your perspective in life determines your response to life itself. You must make a conscience decision to be positive and optimistic in life or you will live and consequently die with a bad reputation. It will be very difficult for anyone to say something good about you. Perspective is crucial to everything we encounter in life. What you see depends on what you are looking for. We must be careful not to see what we want to see. Everyone deserves to receive the benefit of the doubt. It will change your entire outlook in any situation. Optimism says, "See the good", and Pessimism says, "See the bad, the worst". Choose to see the good. And when you see the bad, just keep in mind, nagging, arguing, and harboring bitterness is not the answer and will not resolve the problem. Understanding, compassion, mercy, grace, and forgiveness will help resolve a bone of contention. Everyone needs that at times. This is the part of give and take in a relationship that sometimes taste bitter but can yield fruitful rewards in the end.

Donna Ritchie

6

Leave and Cleave

Genesis 2:24 says, "Therefore shall a man leave his mother and father and cleave to his wife; and they shall be one flesh." Marriage is a union between one man and one woman. In a marriage, it is imperative that you keep your union between the two of you. As much as you love Mom, Dad, and family, your relationship journey primarily exists in the confines of the two of you. I have met countless couples who are struggling with the fact their parents are ruining their marriage. They try to find out what is going on in your relationship and/or in your house. They try to advise you on how to man handle your husband or how to treat your wife. This is a no- no, especially if it will damage your relationship. They even try to tell you how you are to raise your children. There is a thin line between being helpful and being nosey in this kind of situation.

May I tell you a secret? No one has to know what is going on in your relationship or your house unless you tell them. Now I understand parents love their children and sometimes it is difficult to let them go, but when they get married it is time to let them go. Where the problem begins is when the parent or someone outside of your union/your relationship over steps their boundaries and tries to control the relationship. They want to continue being the mother, father, or manager in the relationship. I believe that is why the Bible clearly states a man should leave his mother and father and cleave to his wife. Since the two become one, that leaves no room for a third party. It does not state the three becomes one or the four becomes one, it states the two become one. If you do not do this it has been proven to be a challenge in a relationship. Some people and yes in some cases, family members, aim to break up your relationship for the wrong reason. This is absolutely wrong. Let no man put asunder, meaning do not let anyone break up your union. That is why marriage is a major decision never to be taken lightly. When you decide to marry, there are boundaries drawn by the two of you and no one can over step unless you allow them to. There are places in marriage no one should be involved in but the two involved in the relationship.

Here is some helpful advice in dealing with your family. If your parents are living in your house, whether it is physically or verbally, and it is a problem for your spouse, you are to deal with your parent or loved ones. Why? Because when you deal with them, there is no real love loss however, if your spouse has to deal with them, there can and will be a love loss factor there. Most people really want to get along however.....sometimes that may not be the case. When you got married, you really married your spouse not his or her family. Their family is a part of their life and that is wonderful, however, they are not your spouse. Therefore your dealings are with your spouse. If his or her family becomes too involved in your relationship to where it is causing problems, you (the off spring to the parent) should handle your own family. When your spouse is uncomfortable with your family, then you should take your extended family matters into your hands and handle it. It is unfair to your spouse for them to handle it, granted they probably can take care of the situation, but one of the worst positions to be in, is in between your spouse and his or her family in a negative way.

Husbands and wives, stop telling those outside of your union about your marriage, especially those things called problems, discrepancies, and character flaws. When the time comes for advice or counseling, consult someone who is wise and unbiased; someone who will not have ill feelings towards your spouse once the dust simmers. Someone who will not rehash your situation to you or anyone else. The Bible describes it as seeking wise counsel. Everybody does not give wise counsel so be very careful where you receive counsel. When you receive counsel, an amen corner is not the answer. When you receive counsel, 'the right' corner is necessary for answers. You want to get your advice from someone who will tell you what is absolutely right whether it places you at fault or not.

You want someone who clearly sees both sides to your story. I'm not saying someone who will be brutal with you, but someone who will constructively advise you and your problem. That is why public disagreements between two unbending people are useless. When you really want answers, you get to the bottom of things and get them. However you must be willing to see yourself and how you play a part in it as well.

I am convinced when you do things God's way, you get His results. In a relationship it is wonderful to see two people interact with each other. It is good to see two mature people iron out their differences. Your difference and the fact that you came to some agreement, becomes a milestone to note. When you're able to get past it and still get along, that is what makes you qualified to disagree without being disagreeable. That is what makes the boys, men and the girls, women. That is when maturity arrives and immaturity vanishes.

In a relationship there are enough problems you will have to deal with without having your extended loved ones interfere. If you placed a couple on an island alone, there would still be something to deal with. My advice to extended loved ones and parents of a couple: allow them the space they need to become one together. More than anything they would like to know you love the both of them. Be there if they really need you and if you render your advice give them loving, unbiased, wise, and helpful advice. Support and bless their union, respect them, their union, and if there are children involved, highly regard their way of raising their children, especially when it is in accordance to God's word and simply morally right. If it is not a Biblical sin or something that will kill them, then support and respect their method of their relationship and child rearing. There is not a perfect antidote to a relationship or child rearing. It is simply trial and error, live and learn.

To the parents of a married couple, please know your kids love you and they sometimes request your advice. They want you in their lives, but understand your place and the boundaries and do not overstep them because that is when problems occur. Living and learning life together has its highs and lows. It may mean falling down and scraping your knee but you get up and try it again together. The thorns in life are there to help us appreciate the rose it will produce. Every couple needs room to grow together.

It is gratifying to know if you need your parents or loved ones that they are there unconditionally to support you and your family. The wonderful thing about being married is sharing your life and its details with your spouse; the one you love. Love your life, embrace it, the good and the not so good experiences, and make the best of everything. It can be done. Live on the bright side of life.

Donna Ritchie

7

Committed For Life

Marriage Lifetime Chart

Estimate Time Table		
Discovering Individuality	0-7 years	Getting to know you
Adjustments	8-14 years	Now that you are familiar with one another, work it for two while being happy. Compliment and Affirm your relationship
Settle In and Enjoy	15 plus years	Have fun together. Encourage your individuality

Love is the foundation for building a successful relationship

Discover your mate. Find your relational
rhythm and what it takes to make your
relationship work.

Now that you have found what makes your relationship work. Work it with pleasure. It is wonderful to be into each other.

Settle in and enjoy each other. Do fun things together and create your own memories.

Donna Ritchie

8

Discovering Your Individuality

It is important to get to know your partner. In the process of knowing your partner, it is strongly advised that you handle this process with great consideration for each other, never taking one another for granted. Never assume you know him or her to the fullest. Be mindful and careful of how you speak to one another. Calm approach to any situation resolves quicker than hostile approach. Hostile approach creates a defensive response. Jumping to conclusions is an absolute no-no. Typically during the first years of marriage, particularly the first 7 years, are the times when two people who are in love and gotten married rediscover their individuality.

After the bliss of being in love and adjusting to married life, common reality sets in, the masks peel off, and all pretense is dissolved. The real "you" is the focus; the real "you" is at the forefront. Now it is time to work on yourself to adjust to your mate, meaning knowing who you are and working your individuality into your mate's individuality to make a whole union.

The one myth that destroys relationships is the notion to change someone else. This is the biggest mistake one can make. No one likes to change and especially change into a robot for you or anyone. In relationships this is where you are allowed to be who you are and still love and be loved. The best antidote for change is to allow God to change your partner. It amazes me. Each time a change needs to be made and after consulting God, the Creator of all things, He always addresses the one requesting change. He shines the light on the one needing change, first. It is only wise that after catching on to His plan that we redirect our prayers to focus on ourselves first and carefully examine what you are doing or what have you said to aid in the problem and patiently allow Him to work on the other person. Each time He will come through for you. See, what we fail to realize in praying for our mate is, 'God loves them too', and He has their best interest at heart too. He knows them better than we do. He knows their intent when we don't have a clue. He sees and knows beyond what we think, we see, and know of our mate.

No one can make you lose your cool, you give it away. No one can make you lose your temper, you give it away. Often times you give it away for lack of understanding. You want to know how to win more bees? With honey. The Bible talks about, "With love and kindness have I drawn thee". With love and kindness God drew you and guess what? With love and kindness you can win more battles than none. Love never fails.

Understand the first years of marriage are critical to the longevity of your relationship. It determines the level of trust your relationship will be based on. Often times those things that you did not notice before you got married was because you were in love and all shook up. Some of those questionable things you saw, they usually do not go away because you get married. Sometimes they even get worse but when you willfully say, "Yes, I'll marry you", you agree to the fact that, "Yes, I_am willing to deal with it." Now granted there are things you cannot see until you get married however, in your observation keep in mind your mate will be observing you and they are observing things about you as well. Marriage is not about finding fault and discrepancies of which you will become aware of some faults. It is about two people in love and wanting to spend the rest of their lives ENHANCING and AFFIRMING their love. Enhancing and affirming to you and your mate's happiness and satisfaction should be in the forefront of your endeavors to making your relationship work best for the two of you. In the Old Testament, when two people were married it was custom for them to spend the first year together. If there was a war, the husband could not go. This was time for them to get to know one another first before embarking on anything else. Getting to know your mate is so important. It takes a lifetime to get to know someone but for one year they had to get adjusted to being married. Before you win others you must first win your own. You know you are all that and a bag of chips when publicly you are as good as gold and privately your mate thinks you are too.

Since we are surrounded by so much negative publicity in marriage, I would like to challenge you to commit to the following:

Change your negative thinking to positive thinking

Be optimistic – at all times

See how less you can argue/disagree

Learn to disagree without being disagreeable

Always THINK before you SPEAK

Have fun, don't be so serious all the time

Enhance and celebrate your relationship, your life together

Remember God has your partner's best interest too

Be an effective team player

Always concentrate and highlight the bright side, the positives

A good marital relationship means two people being open to one another which causes you to become vulnerable to one another. Being vulnerable is normal in marital relationships that is what makes marriage a committed union. There is no one else in the world you should be more opened with than your spouse. That is why disagreements and subsequent divorces are so harsh, hurtful, and filled with extreme rage and revenge. However, it is mandatory of you to handle your mate with extreme care at all times. The word optimistic means hoping for the best, seeing the best. Everyone wishes for his or her best to be seen at all times. Listen with your optimistic ears and with ALL of your getting. In life, please get a good, clear understanding before you say a word and when angry, know the facts first before you fly off the handle, before you react. It is sad to say, often times a hostile negative reaction derives from a person with a pessimistic hearing aid, blinders on, and who jumps to the wrong conclusion. A good listener carefully processes information before he or she utters a word. Stop assuming the worst and flying off the handle when you're angry. For peace sake, stop bringing up dirty laundry that should have been settled a long time ago. No one living in a glass house should throw stones. Sometimes when you know the facts, when you understand the reasoning behind a situation whether its outcome is good or bad, it helps your perspective and reaction to it. We all have faults however, the Bible says, "Love covers a multitude of sin". Learn to appreciate your differences. Stop tripping over your differences. Think about this, if your mate was just like you, you could not stand it. You would absolutely hate it. Sometimes we cannot stand ourselves, sometimes we do not understand ourselves. I encourage you to appreciate your differences. Use your differences as a means to make your relationship whole, better, and to enhance your relationship. Look at your differences as a means of seeing the whole picture as you learn and consider the other side of the situation.

There are times the two of you will not view a situation from the same perspective. That doesn't mean you pull out the boxing gloves. That does not mean you get a divorce and that does not mean you have to say anything especially if the outcome is not going to kill you. Thank God you do not think alike. Thank God you are different. That is what makes you whole. That is the 'becoming' you vowed on your wedding day. One day the two of you will start to think alike without saying a word. You will astound one another because you did.

Opposites really do attract and make a whole. Two individuals 'becoming' one means you pick up where I leave off and guess what? We both win. We both shine. The two of you have created 'Your Relational Rhythm'. There are no two people alike on this planet. Thank God. We all were fearfully and wonderfully made. Now, if we can turn our differences into something positive and something to grow on, we will lower the divorce rates tremendously. We will have more couples loving each other out of pure desire and not out of force.

Everyone has to adjust to something. Allow your mate to be an individual and adjust yourself. You might have to reposition yourself but only to better your relationship together. Find out what works for the two of you and work it. Your relationship and your mate reflect 'You', your choice, and your taste. When they are happy, it makes them look good and it makes you look superb! People will love to see you coming. The important thing is making each other happy because you love one another. The Bible talks about marriage and always refers to Christ and His relationship to the Church. He always enhances the Church. He always speaks well of Her. He is a life giver. He sees the great potential and always speaks it over the church, His Bride. He believes and confesses great things even when it is not evident. We should always do the same. Listen, faith comes by hearing and hearing by the word of God. Be relentless in speaking good things over your mate. Be known as a positive, refreshing force in your relationship and the true test of being positive is not just being positive under positive conditions, but being positive in negative situations. When things aren't going well your being positive in a negative situation speaks volumes to all involved whether it is voiced or not. You want others to speak well of you? Then give them reason to speak well of you. Give them something great to say about you by being great. My Mama always taught me, "If you don't have anything nice to say then don't say anything at all." I realize there is not a perfect human in this world, but there are those who aspire to do well in life and in their aspiration the good out shines the bad.

Donna Ritchie

9

Adjusting To Your Relationship

Now that you have discovered your individuality and have learned to work with and appreciate certain attributes of your mate, it is time to be okay. You have found what works and what does not work for you and your mate and you are now working together. You began to appreciate your differences and love it because you do not want to be living and sleeping with a robot. Every relationship has its rhythm. The two of you are now adjusting to the rhythm of your relationship. Keep working it and making your own music. Keep doing what works best for the two of you. Do not allow anyone or anything to interfere or destroy your beat. See, in your relational rhythm, it is a beat that the two of you are happy with and have come to terms with. It makes the both of you happy, satisfied, and closer. As you work it, you are building a trust that will be strong. You are redefining your love that was not only founded on a deep feeling, but now a love which roots go much deeper. Your relationship is more interesting, intriguing, and exciting because now you are discovering one another. Your relationship is on another level now. You have gotten in touch with one another's heart. You discover what makes them tick and what makes them tock. You have learned and continued to learn to listen to their heart regardless of what is said or done. You are understanding why and how they do what they do. When you understand a person's heart, you understand them better. In a relationship you will always learn, discover, rediscover, adapt, and adjust. It is a life- long lesson till death do you part. It makes life so interesting. It is the art of love. Love is a powerful thing. It endures and when love endures it has gone beyond a feeling and has graduated to an action; a commitment. Endured love sees the good potential in everything even in the not so good setting. God sees the good in you even when you weren't so good. Love is something EVERYONE needs including Mr. Rascal and Mrs. Sassy.

10

Settle In and Enjoy

This is the time to really make the most of your relationship. You have recognized your differences and have found a way to make it work for your good. Your relational rhythm is beating. It's working now. This is the time when you have done your homework and the two of you know one another in a good general sense. It is time to enjoy one another. By this time you should know what your mate likes and dislikes. You should know the intricate details of each other. You should know your husband likes his coffee dark with a teaspoon of hazelnut cream and a cinnamon Danish on the side. And for additives, you know how it turned him on when you served it to him in your sexy lingerie and how it puts a pep in his step. You should know and remember how your wife thought it was so nice of you to make up the bed. She loved the red rose you gave her on Mother's day and she thought it was extra special that you placed a rose on her pillow. She loved it enough that she went an extra mile and turned on her charm for you. These are the things you have already taken notes on throughout the years you've been together. These are the things you are doing at this point in your relationship...just because. Making each other's day, spending your time charming one another rather than challenging each other, relishing your relationship, and complimenting one another verbally and in your actions. There comes a time in every relationship where you settle in and kill the competition, the rivalry among yourselves. In life, 'growing older is mandatory and growing up is optional.' Yes, when you first started out you had to learn how to speak to each other and treat each other. It is like a child. You start out with incoherent speech but as you grow older and grow up, your speech and your behavior changes and improves. Your understanding becomes enlightened and enriched.

Marital relationships should get better with time. The reason you bump heads particularly on the front end of the relationship is because you have two individuals trying to become one; trying to put their puzzle pieces together. There are no two pieces alike. With time you learn what pieces go where and how the two can work together to become one puzzle. Again, this is synonymous with the saying, "Two becoming one". When the two of you understand your place, your rhythm, and who brings what to your table of life together, the puzzle pieces called, 'your individual lives' start to connect and work together. Then you start to compliment your individuality.

Working together in a relationship is two individual people with different viewpoints, ideas, and opinions creating a common bond. Mature people learn how to focus on the positives and work to bring out the good of the other to make the two become an awesome whole. Your relationship will not only excite the two of you but it will become an inspiration to other relationships and to those who are contemplating relationship. This is what I mean by 'settling in and enjoying'. You conscientiously reflect on the love that brought you together and keep building on that.

Can you do it with children, the cat, and the dog around? Yes! Children need to see Mom and Dad hold hands every now and then. They need to see Mom and Dad have fun together and laugh. Then there is a time to put the children to bed early. Sometimes you may have to take a break and let the children spend the night at Grandma's or a trusted friend's house. You might have to put the cat and dog out. But spend some quality time together and create memories that only you and your spouse can share together; something for the two of you to make goo- goo eyes at one another and laugh about. You owe it to one another and the children. Learn to have fun together and do not take life so serious. Live and be happy while you're living. You only have one life to live, live it to the fullest and enjoy it while God has blessed you to have it.

I always like the notion of making life so good for my husband that is hard for a third party to fit in. You should make your spouse's life so good and refreshing that they would not want to wander off. They really enjoy you and what you are all about. How do you do that? I'm so glad you asked, by being positive, optimistic, by being fun to be around, by always speaking positive things over your mate and your children, by living and staying on the bright side of life. When you begin to do this it makes your life much better. You will be surprised at how your blood pressure will go down.

You will take years off your appearance. It reduces the headaches. In order to do this you must decide to 'Live on the Bright Side' of life.

By this time in life you are aware of your spouse's heart. You know when they are quiet at home, that they are not mad at you but maybe they just need some quiet time after being at work all day. Give it to them. When you know their heart you can understand good days and bad days better. If they 'go off' you will know not to become quick to the draw but you can try to understand why they are going off and you can deal with it calmly.

Love is two people enjoying and enhancing one another

You can give them space and not go into it at all. You can be there for them and make the rest of their day better with a massage or something that will impress them. Sometimes people need to let off steam and need an ear to listen. Learn how to not be so quick to the draw when there is a cranky moment. Learn how to keep a cool head when there is room for disagreement. When you are at the 'settling in' years and enjoying it, you affirm, affirm, and affirm your relationship in innovative ways. If it is the little foxes that spoil the vine, make those same little foxes behave for your good. All it takes is a little spark to start a fire. It takes those little sparks to keep the fires burning. Be creative in your pursuit for a positive, exciting, loving lifestyle. Turn on the romance, pump up and magnify the good things in your spouse. Keep the excitement in your relationship. Ecstasy in a relationship never hurt anyone. It keeps the family together and your children can keep a good foundation in life. They will relish the fact that Mom and Dad love each other. It is such a good solid foundation for them and a great life for you.

Stay in love with each other. I challenge you to see how well you can get along. See how less you can argue and disagree. See how positive and loving you can be. Men, let the Macho Lover come out of you and ladies, the queen or the princess in you, make her come out and 'let down her hair' while she's out. Turn on the charm and hold on to it tightly as you run with it. Men, flex those chest muscles or if they have fallen south, then flex those eyebrows. Ladies, tease to please. Tantalize like you did when you were dating. Flirt, flirt, and then flirt.

It is amazing that when you observe a crowd of people, you can always spot those couples who are single and those who are married. The single couples are lovey- dovey. They are stuck to one another like glue. However, the married couples seem to see which side of the world they can walk furthest from one another. Here's a news flash, married couples, you are legal. Don't be ashamed of your love for one another. You can cuddle. Holding hands, hugging, and laughing is neither a sin nor a disease. You're married now. You can do it. Single couples should only remind you of how it use to be when you were single. Their cuddling should cause you to wonder where in life did the two of you get off the love boat? No matter the reason, get back on the love boat and stay there. Keep the love flames lit. Do whatever it takes to keep the wood turning so the fire will not go out of your relationship. Here are some ideal activities you can do together:

Go for a walk, holding hands.

Go to the movies (a movie both will enjoy).

Visit a fun park and go racecar driving.

Play Boggles or a game of your choice.

Share a sweet treat.

Go for a romantic drive in your car.

Enjoy quiet time in your own backyard.

Talk about silly, fun things.

Laugh, laugh, play, and laugh some more.

Get involved in a competitive activity where you are on the same side.

The list can go on and on. Often times when you sit back and observe your partner you will be amazed at the good things you will learn. You discover what he or she likes and enjoys. You will discover when they are with their friends what makes them laugh or why they enjoy their friends so much. Maybe you should do some of the things their friends do. I had a friend tell me, "Every time you and my wife get together, you are always laughing. She never laughs as much around me." That is a great time to find out what makes one laugh so much. Find out why do they hang out together especially if it is a decent place to hang out. Find out where they are hanging out together. If it is the mall, maybe you should go to the mall with them sometimes. If it is at the golf course, maybe you should go golfing. You should be interested in their life because you love them. Do not do it for spying or controlling purposes. This kind of behavior only infuriates the other. Those days are over by now. You are now in the days of rolling out the red carpet for one another. Enhancing one another's life is a given by now. The two should be competing on how to over exceed the other in enhancing each other. God created marriage to be fun not boring.

11

Couples with Children

Parents must be carefully aware of what is said and done in the company of children. Children are like sponges. They soak up their surroundings especially those in the confines of their home. Children do what they see, not necessarily what they are told. Parents set the atmosphere in their home. Parents should not argue in front of their children. Why? It disrupts the environment. It contaminates the atmosphere. You are the foundation in their life and arguing shakes their foundation. Responsible parents disagree behind closed doors. Often times children witness adult problems and consequentially their process is that of a child. They are not familiar with the magnitude of adult disagreements. It is a huge deal for children because it involves the two people they love most. Believe it or not, a child's perception of their parents is so colossal it is unbelievable. Whether your child looks or responds accordingly, your relationship REALLY effects them to the uttermost. Parenting give security, stability, and completion in a child's life, just to name a few. Maybe you are contentiously married, separated, or divorced, however, when you disagree or when there is contention in your relationship it scars the child. It hurts them beyond their imagination. Stop arguing and having ill vibes in the company of your children by all means necessary. Strive to keep the atmosphere at an even keel in the presence of children. Be an adult. Be a responsible parent and disagree somewhere else.

If you do not believe me when I say parenting impacts your child and what you do and say as a parent does not affect your child, watch their behavior. They will either withdraw in fear or they will strongly rebel. Why? Because they are trying to process an adult situation from a minor's perspective. It is like trying to feed an infant T-bone steak. It is too much and too thick for them to handle and they will have a very difficult time processing it. That is why when children become adults they often times repeat what they have seen at home, good or bad because they are a product of their environment. As a parent, it is only wise to make life better for our children. It helps them tremendously both personally and in their interaction with others. Life alone has its highs and lows. It is not necessary for adults to make it more difficult for them. However, it is wonderful to see them grow into responsible, loving adults.

You will be amazed at how much your children are just like you. My question to you. What kind of person are you? Pay attention to other's perception of you. If they generally observe a particular character trait in you, maybe it is something you will want to consider and ponder. Children do what they see in most parent -child relationships. There are some great parents who do an absolute fine job of raising their children. The legendary Bill Cosby once said, "Great parents are made by great children."

This is what disagreeing does to a child or anyone outside of your relationship. It forces them to feel trapped and brutally effected by your words and behavior.

Donna Ritchie

12

Knowing Who You Are

The saying, "You are product of your environment", speaks volumes in good or bad behavior in children. Children are unknowingly vulnerable. Particularly in a separation or divorce situation, they become aware of their vulnerability. The foundation they were born into has been torn or utterly destroyed which causes a process of reaction. It devastates them. On the other hand, there are children who relish the idea of wanting to be like their Mom and Dad with a pleasant glow in their expression. I believe children unconsciously understand balance. It is the imbalances in life that become difficult to conceive and ultimately process. In the processing stage it ultimately comes out in various forms. Some forms are deep depression, withdrawals, and sometimes thoughts of suicide.

I know we are talking about parenting however, it is also challenging for adults to be in the company of couples who argue and those who stink up the atmosphere with attitudes and disagreements. It is bad enough to verbally disagree but it is equally uncomfortable to be in the company of the silent disagreement. No one wishes to be around anyone arguing and fussing. The Bible even admonishes us to not deal with an angry man. Do you want to know why sometimes people leave and don't return or are withdrawn and have very few words to say? Sometimes it is you and before they hear or engage in another disagreement with you, they would rather leave or not say anything at all. This is an extremely uncomfortable, unpleasant life for the victim. Uncomfortable because they wish to be open and honest with you, but if it is at the expense of a lecture, a guilt trip, or an argument, they would rather not say or do anything. They would rather keep the peace. However, everyone needs to communicate and if they cannot communicate with you, then they will do one of two things. They will go to someone else who will listen to them and not give them any backlash or they will keep it all in and become a walking time bomb ready to explode at any given time. What a terrible life to have to live. Life does not have to be this way. Why not dare to be different and make life much better for yourself and your loved one?

Here's where if you want your relationship to work, you must adhere to and keep in mind. You cannot just say nor do anything to your partner. Be quick to hear and slow to speak. Be slow to wrath. You will be surprised at what you will learn. Words are those things, once out, they can never be retrieved. When we stand before a holy and righteous God, we are going to be judged for what we say and what we do. When God's word said this, it did not specify to whom or with whom. He said He would judge us by what we say (Matt 12:36) and what we do (Col 3:23-25). With this in mind, I believe you will be more careful of your behavior.

Don't you know God loves that person you are cussing out? He loves that person you are giving a hard time, just as He loves you. He is also watching and listening. Just as God is a comforter, with consistent misbehavior in word or deed, He will become your judge. You must be careful. The thing that impacted my interaction with my husband at the beginning of our marriage and till this day is God reminding me ,"He that winneth souls is wise." 'He has a soul' and there is no way I can effectively win others to Christ and not my husband. Yes, even though he has accepted Jesus Christ, he still has to be won to Christ. Your lifestyle can either turn someone else onto Christ or it can turn them off to Christ.

To think you can win and impress others and neglect your spouse and your children is a warped and dysfunctional mindset. Some say, "He or she made me do it". "They made me mad and I lost control". People in general and life itself will lend you many opportunities to blow your cool, but you don't 'go off' at every whim. To say you lost control, reality says you gave it away. Stop giving yourself away. No one can make you lose control, you choose to give it away. Once gone, the damage done can be irreplaceable or can take years to mend.

I remember the day after getting married I thought, "What next?" We have one another now. I was afraid of boredom. I was afraid of marriage because of what people were telling me it was like. It is simply profound when God speaks to you because not only do you understand the face value of what He says but often times the meaning goes much deeper than what is actually said. I remember God telling me, "Act like you are girlfriend and boyfriend." It was the mindset of a girlfriend and boyfriend. Think about your position when you were dating. You cherished and enjoyed each other's company and you expressed good positive feelings. The atmosphere was peaceful and pleasant. You put on your best behavior suit and wore it out. You impressed for success!

To have a good relationship, you should remember to keep and use your good manners. Conscientiously focus on the good things in your partner. No one wants his or her faults magnified. It is natural for us to gravitate to good things. We all want our goodness highlighted. Everyone likes to be celebrated. If you want good things then you have to give out good things. 'You win more flies with honey than with vinegar'. The best way to do that is 'do good because you want to.' Since you know you are so good, wholesome, and pleasant, "To the pure all things are pure," let your entire goodness and wholesomeness spill out onto your partner and your loved ones. What are you saving it for? Do unto others as you would have them do unto you. You reap what you sow. Love your neighbor as you love yourself. I love what Gomer Pyle would always say, " Look on the bright side!" This statement is powerfully true. If you look on the bright side it makes for a good, positive, and optimistic life.

It is amazing that children do what they see. It is important they know Mom and Dad love one another and have fun together. It makes their world much more stable and secure. Nowadays that is so critical in their upbringing. It is the positive things you do as parents that impact them for the rest of their lives. The negative imprints in their lives will make them either become the monster they saw in their parents or run as far away from their perception of what they saw in their parents. Children look up to their parents with so much vulnerability in their eyes. We owe it to them to be the very best parents we can be so when they become parents of your grandchildren they will be great parents to them as well.

Children need to have more positive influences in their lives. The imbalances come in part because there is too much of one side of life. In order to live a balanced life in an unbalanced world, they equally need to see both sides of parental training. For example, when you, the parent, reprimand them they need to see the loving, cuddling, hugging side of you as much as they see the other side of you. I would like to say they need to see the loving, cuddling side of you more. This helps them understand you better and why you disciplined them. Communication is key in relationships. Here again, with all your getting in life, get an understanding. When you understand people, particularly your loved ones, you deflate stress, unhappiness, feelings of discomfort, unrest, and tension.

Make life pleasant so others will want to be around you. Make it peaceable enough that your children, your spouse can come and talk to you and feel good about it and not walk away feeling inadequate or stupid.

Be mindful of your expression, your voice tone, and your body language all of which plays a very important role in whether or not you are the one to talk to or be around. I like the GEICO commercial that says, "We all do dumb things." The words used and the voice tone is amazing. A dumb thing is a dumb thing and we all are guilty of doing something dumb. Keeping that in mind is essential. It doesn't make you dumb, it just says the thing you did was not the best choice you have made. But get up, dust yourself off, and try again. You are smarter and better than that. You are special indeed. It is time others become aware of the good you really possess. It is useless if you are the only one who knows it. Let others know it as well.

13

The Power Of Agreement

When two come together and agree, things happen. When you and your spouse agree on something like having a great evening together, you commit to a great evening and it happens, right? Just think when you set your mind to doing something good. How does it make you feel? In a relationship it is important that you agree. The longer you are in a relationship, it is crucial to agree more often than you disagree. Now let's understand why sometimes we disagree as a whole whether it is with your spouse or with anyone. When you disagree you must realize first of all that the two of you are individuals with your very own ideas and opinion. There are no two people alike. It is okay to disagree, just don't allow your disagreement to make you disagreeable people. You cannot force your idea or opinion on anyone. Think about it for a minute. What makes you so right? Even if you are right, everyone is entitled to his or her opinion. This subject may seem petty but in relationships you will be amazed at how much people argue over something they do not agree upon and will get mad and not speak for days, weeks, and even months. They will sleep in separate rooms, avoid one another, and some are ready to tangle over nothing. My challenge to you is to learn to appreciate and see the good in disagreeing. You would not want a 'yes' man or woman would you? It is okay to give your partner room to disagree.

Think about this example. When the two of you commit to raising your child, each parent has his or her own way of raising that child. Your husband may not comb your little daughter's hair like you do, but let him comb her hair especially if he doesn't mind doing so. He's being the man and taking care of her. Ladies want their man to be the man but at the same time shoot him down for being the man. Why? Because his version of being a man may be different from your version of what a man is to be like. You want your man to be the head of your home but at the same time you strip him with your mouth of his position. You criticize the way he makes up your bed or the way he helps you fold the clothes. By the time you finish degrading him for his efforts, he feels deflated and is not motivated to ever help you again or sometimes he is not even motivated to wearing the pants in his own home. Whether you realize it or not, you have created your own problem. Now he does not want to be around you because you tear him down. He does not want to help around the house because all he hears is your constant nagging him. In my example, I have used a woman versus a man, but this goes both ways. Let me ask you ladies. What is your version of a man in his home? Men, what is your version of a woman in her home? The answer is, "No one knows." Each makes up its own version and with communication each enhances the other.

I am trying to get you to think before you say or do something that does not produce anything good. When two people strongly disagree to the point of getting utterly mad and totally disagreeable, there are several elements involved. The first thing is to realize that you have two people who are trying to force their individual ideas on the other which is extremely unpleasant to the other and in most cases, unsuccessful in their attempt. They are inconsiderate of their counterpart. Hebrews 10:24 tells us to, "Consider one another". When you do not consider your brother or sister, you lose their respect and tamper with their trust in you. Sometimes even if they are wrong and you are right, wouldn't it be better to waive your rights, especially if it is not going to kill you and win their respect in you for respecting their decision to disagree with you in the long run? I think it is wonderful to have a human being living, breathing, and sleeping beside me rather than a robot. A robot is a machine that is programmed to think and act like you. A robot is a lifeless piece of metal. Robots are not even human.

Is this you or your partner?

They do not have feelings, view points, ideas, or opinions. They react and respond because they are forced to, not because they want to or even desire to do something. They do not smile; they have a lifeless, plastered smile on their face. They are not happy. Isn't that a cold description of someone being forced to be something they are not? It also describes one being controlled by another person. 'Robots' know if they do not think and act like you, there are unpleasant consequences.

Robots do not have a life in and of themselves. They are simply a cold piece of programmed metal. There is not a human being on this planet that wishes or even aspires to be a robot. It is so easy and life is so much better when we are allowed to be ourselves. When in a relationship, most people are in it because they feel special by the other. They are validated; they are loved unconditionally. It is crucial to constantly express love and validation for the longevity sake of the marriage.

Practice agreeing together on a daily basis. The act alone will create a bond much deeper than the deed itself. There are good deeds in life to follow for what it does on a deeper level than the formality of doing it. In other words, the positive things you say and do go much deeper in a relationship. It forms a bond and creates personal treasures that money cannot buy; that words cannot express.

14

Consider the Cause

It is mandatory to consider, to carefully think about what you say and do to others. It determines the kind of reaction you receive. Every reaction begins with an action. There are some things that if said would really hurt us. Like telling your mate, "I need my space". Instead, spare the harsh words and feelings and just give it to them. Offer it to them because in time you will need some space as well. Allow your spouse some 'me time' especially when you know they are really trying to be a good husband or wife. Give your spouse the freedom of being themselves. Let them be their own individual self without having to demand it by verbal or physical means. So many people leave relationships because they are not allowed to be themselves. Instead of living with someone they love to be around, they live with a dictator. No one wants to be controlled or dictated to in his or her own home. Home is a place where one can be comfortable and loved unconditionally. To disagree without being disagreeable is a learned behavior. You can disagree and still get along. Instead of disagreeing all the time learn to agree more often. Two people agreeing feels better and its outcome yields long lasting good results.

Disagreements like this can be resolved immediately. Next time, he should remember to speak . Additionally, she has to grow up, mature, and understand her happiness is important to him whether he speaks or not. He probably had something on his mind.

How do you disagree without being disagreeable? I'm so glad you asked. When there is a disagreement between the two of you, first of all calm down. Cool off if you're angry. Carefully consider one another and try to understand each side of the story before you proceed. Secondly, do not allow your private problems to become public property. In other words, when you disagree, do not disagree in front of others. Concentrate on getting to the solution; get to the answer. Getting to the answer is excluding all others and in the privacy of your place, room, or wherever the two of you can be alone, resolve your issues and when the discussion of over, then it's over never to be brought up again because it's over.

When you disagree in front of others it then involves others. Disagreement effects others. This behavior does not resolve what is going on between the two of you. It makes others uncomfortable. It showcases dirty laundry that no one else should know about. It highlights the aggressor's immaturity and makes you look bad. Just as it causes your health to deteriorate, your stress level to increase, and your stomach to hurt, it causes other's health to deteriorate as well. When you disagree, deal with it by all means necessary and get over it. Do not bring it up again. Get rid of the old laundry right then and there. Stop bringing up old laundry. How would you like it if each time you did something wrong God brought up your old laundry after you have repented of it? When you harbor resentment it makes your blood pressure rise. As funny as it sounds, I've heard people say, "Ooh, he or she makes my blood boil!" It causes your heartbeat to rise, gives you ulcers, and you lose sleep. That is why God's word tells us in Ephesians 4:26, "Don't let the sun go down on your wrath", and in Romans 12: 17-18, "As much as it is within you, you are to live peaceably with each other." Unresolved issues are bad for your health.

Proverbs 21:19 says, "It is better to dwell in the wilderness than with a contentious and angry woman." Proverbs 25:24 states, "It is better to dwell in the corner of the housetop, than with a brawling woman and in a wide house." Typically women are characterized as the ones who nag however, there are men who nag also. Perhaps we will paraphrase that to say a nagging man or woman. Nagging is a steady stream of unwanted advice and is a form of torture. People nag because they think they are not getting through but nagging hinders communication more than it helps. When you are tempted to engage in this destructive, habit-forming behavior, stop and examine your motives. Are you more concerned about yourself? Are you more concerned about getting your way? Are you engulfed in being right than about the person you are pretending to help? If you are truly concerned about other people, there is a more effective way to get through to them. Surprise them with words of love and patience and see what happens.

Often times when I see couples arguing and airing dirty laundry on each other, I think to myself, "That is information overload. That's too much info; more than anyone cares to know." Don't misunderstand my next statement because if you did not 'go off', then this information would not have been a topic of discussion. However, it makes you wonder about the one 'going off'. If he or she were not here, we would have never known this information. Whether you realize it or not, people are not interested in you airing your problems especially if you are doing it just because you can or because you are trying to make a point to the one you're arguing with. That should be dealt with privately behind your closed doors. Some may say, "Well, you just don't understand my situation". And we may not understand it directly if we have not gone through it with that person however, there are similar situations in our lives that yield the same outcome. On the flip side, your spouse might be reacting harshly to you because of your behavior.

Then it brings to mind the notion, I wonder how did they fall in love in the beginning? Surely it was not like this.

Anger is like a fire out of control and it burns you and everything in its path. It divides people. That's why when you want to really get to the crust of the problem, you don't air it in front others and especially those who cannot help you. You deal with it among yourself and if it does not get resolved, you get help and seek wise counseling. Anger can be a legitimate reaction to injustice but you must also consider, what caused it? Are you reacting to an evil situation that you are going to set right? Or are you responding selfishly to a personal insult? Anger is something that must be controlled at all times. You have to look at the constructive and destructive aspect of your anger. Sometimes you will have to waive your rights; take a chill pill for peace sake. What I am simply saying is examine yourself when you are angry. You must ponder the question within yourself after you have calmed down and that question is, "What makes you so right?" Suppose you are wrong? I encourage you to always carefully think before you turn on the faucet because words are those things that once out, they are out. It is then you will wonder why no one wants to open up to you; no one wishes to be around you. They shun you like the plague. Then you have created your own problem and the very thing you've always wanted, like the two of you being together, you have now ran them away from you and pushed them either into their friends, their work, or something or someone else.

If you want to get along and have a loving, healthy relationship with your spouse, always remember the day you fell in love. Be mindful of what brought you to this place of a relationship in the first place. Love brought you here and it is love, commitment, and working together (teamwork) that will keep you there. Always remember it takes two halves working together to make a whole. You can do it. All it takes is one step at a time. Step into your relationship on the bright side. You will find your deeds become unconscious habits which will reap a rewarding relationship. Living on the bright side of your relationship will only make your lives better. Why not decide to live a better life and help someone else (your spouse) have a better life? You owe it to yourself and to the one you love.

Teamwork is halves working together and reaching a common goal together

15

Appreciate What You Have

Life is full of valuable things we all need and cannot buy. A healthy relationship is one of those things. Healthy relationships are those that have understanding and wisdom which means common sense and knowledge. Maybe this is your first time in a relationship like the one you're in. If you do not know what you have and you have it, grab a book or magazine, read it, and gain some knowledge on the subject. Get around people you aspire to be like. Get around couples who are positive and love each other. If you want your relationship to be like this, then learn and glean from the best. Practice the attributes you see and like. Try new things.

Learn to appreciate what you have. Nourish it, cherish it, and do not take it for granted and for goodness sake do not lose your respect. When you nourish something, you feed it and take care of it to the best of your ability. Feed your partner good things. You feed them by doing good to them and speaking good things over them, seeing their good qualities, highlighting them, and enhancing their life.

Every day you should appreciate your spouse in some way. When they come home from work, be glad to see them. Be glad to see them in your words, your voice, your tone, and your actions. You should love them so much that you cannot contain yourself. You say it and you show it. Be refreshing to them. Learn how to change hats and character. Be their best friend, be their confidant, and then go in for the kill and be the best lover you can be to them. They will love you all the more for it. When something is wrong surprise them and hit them with a positive, optimistic comeback.

Appreciate them by giving them your undivided attention. A card, a flower, or a balloon just because... is a pleasant gesture. Surprise them with something you know they will like. Ladies, when you do this, it becomes easy for him to love you. It makes him want to work harder just to make you happy. Men, when you do this it is easy for your wife to submit to you. It causes her to go that extra 5 miles to make you happy. She will in turn multiply it back to you. Remember, men are typically ego driven. Why? Because God made them that way and that's okay. Ladies, use it to your advantage and stroke their ego. It's alright to flatter them. Tell your man how wonderful he is. Delilah did it to Samson and it worked. If the 'other' woman knows and can do this, why not you?

The Bible (Prov. 2:16) talks about the 'other' woman. She's described as the 'Strange Woman.' The strange woman is seductive, she wears enticing perfume, she puts on her most persuasive clothing, and she has the latest hairstyle. She flatters her prey. The twinkle in her eye can be seen across the room. Her focus is on her man. Her attitude and mindset is how to entice her prey. She struts like she has it going on and she doesn't care who knows. Ladies, sometimes you have to turn yourself into the other woman and give your man reasons to want to come home. Give him reasons to want to be with you.

Women are emotional. Why? Because God made them that way

and that's okay. Men use it to your advantage and do things that will arouse their emotions like put the kids to bed early and prepare her a warm bath tub of bubbly water with candles surrounding the garden tub...and sometimes jump in it with her. I guarantee you will not hear her complain not one time. Turn on your manly charm. Flex your chest muscles, if you have any left. Romance her verbally and in deed. Make her FEEL like your queen. With women, most things are based on feelings. She has to FEEL. Remove all obstacles that would prevent the two of you from having a wonderful romantic time together. Tell her how much you love her and why you love her. What you say is important but what you do is that much more important to her. Roll out the red carpet for her.

Husbands and wives, you ought to make it easy for your mate to love you by what you say and do for them and with them. With all due respect when someone does something nice and helpful to you, it is a common courtesy to say, "Thank you."

Sometimes as a wife or a husband you feel ashamed and even embarrassed to show affection and express your being into one another. But it is okay for you to show affection. Intimacy is two people into one another. When the two of you are into one another, there is nothing but love and romance, synonymous to nitro and glycerin, joined together to create an explosion. You can do that because you are married now. Get into one another and make your very own relational fireworks.

In relationship it is mandatory to make time to appreciate what you have in one another.

16

You Bring Out The Best In Me

Relationships begin with friendship. Take a minute to think about your best friend and how they make you feel. You feel appreciated, loved, and accepted for who you are and you laugh and have fun together. A friend is someone you aspire to be like in some way. A friend is not someone you fight and argue with all the time. In meaningful relationships, things get better with time. You should bring out the best in one another (the laughter, the peace, the happiness), and the same should be in a marriage relationship. Marriage is a gift and is designed to be exciting, fun, romantic, pleasurable, and full of ectasy. The Bible admonishes husbands to love their wives as they would themselves and as

Christ loves the church. It also states wives are to submit to their own husbands. Can I tell you something? When a man loves a woman, it is easy to submit to him. I am not saying because you feel your husband doesn't love you, you are not to submit. I am simply saying it is easy to love someone who is loveable and easy to submit to someone who loves you. Your goal in your relationship should be to see which of you can out do the other in being the best partner. Go against the grain and be refreshing to your spouse. Bring out the best in your mate. Cover each other. Have each other's best interest at heart. Love one another. Turn on the charm.

The intriguing thing about dating and how loving relationships get started is that they are:

Exciting

Spontaneous

Romantic

Intimate

Delightful to be around

Peaceful

Fun

Optimistic

Positive

Breath taking

Intoxicating

Full of Love

Laughter

Refreshing, and

Full of Suspense.

You must constantly be reminded of the first days when beginning your relationship and how full of bliss it was. Just because you are married does not mean you stop impressing each other. Now that you are married you need to crank up the heat and impress all the more. Take a load off your mind and body and loosen up. Lfe does not have to be so serious. Have fun. Create your own memories. A memory can be something lovely, something fun, something absolutely crazy, or something really heartfelt and warm. Have a rendevous, other than the bedroom, where you and your spouse can devote your undivided attention. I am not talking about sexually, although that's fine too, but a place where the two of you can be alone together. Go for a drive and snuggle. You will be amazed how refreshing and exillarating that is.

Each year around Valentines Day, my husband and I would have a marriage conference at the church we attended. I spoke with the women and he spoke to the men on how we can better our relationships. We would give each married couple homework for one week which culminated into a vacation for them and their spouse. The response was overwhelming. We had couples come up and thank us for the enlightment and the exercises we had them do. We had husbands and wives tell us, "Wow! We have enjoyed what you said. We went home, tried it, and things are so much better now. We have a better understanding of each other now."

Never, ever assume your spouse already knows how you feel about them. You must constantly remind them that, "I Love You." Your spouse is not a mind reader. Open your mouth and say, "I love you, have a nice day, and thank you." After countless comments from various couples, I have come to realize your perspective plays an extremely important role in life and in your interaction with people. Make sure you have an optimistic perception first before your conclusion.

Here are some ideas I encourage you to try for one week with your spouse. If this works, and it will, then you know what you must do from now on.

The Spark Assignment

Day	Assignment
ONLY say and do good, positive, nice things to each other. Compliment and affirm your relationship	
Monday	Write a letter of affirmation to your husband
Tuesday	Write a letter of affirmation to your wife
Wednesday	Give a thoughtful gift to your husband
Thursday	Give a thoughtful gift to your wife
Friday	Have a Romantic Evening
Saturday	Do something fun & romantic with each other

Write a letter of affirmation and tell why you love them. State what they mean to you.

A thoughtful gift can be something bought or something made that you know the other will like.

A romantic evening can be dinner for two, a movie with popcorn, or a walk in the park with ice cream.

Something fun can be a visit to the Fun Park and racing on go-carts. Something romantic can be a drive in the mountains and snuggling in the car.

These are just some examples of what you can do to enhance your relationship. Find out what your mate really likes and aim to please. If this assignment works for you then adhere to it often. Keep the element of surprise churning. Crank up the romance, intimacy, and affection and notice the great subtle changes in your relationship.

When my husband and I conduct Marriage Seminars and the couples did their homework, there were those couples who were very dissatified with their relationship and heading for divorce, however, after completing the homework they came back 2-3 days into the assignment raving about how their relationship is totally new and revived. The husbands would walk in with a bounce in their step, extremely happy, and their wives were ecstatically thrilled at the results in such a short time. They could not wait to get back to doing their homework. It is funny because when they would come to the seminar, you could see the dissatifaction and utter disgust on their faces and when the seminar concluded, you would notice a dramatic difference in their countenance and the awesome intensity of the twinkle in their eye.

Both husband and wife were refreshed, revived, and anticipating more of each other. God intended for marriage to be a fun loving union. Yes, there will be many challenges but that does not mean you have to become two challenging people. Marriage is what you make it. I encourage you to live it up to the fullest.

17

Set The Climate

It is imperative that as a couple you keep the atmosphere pleasant as much and as often as possible. A pleasant, clean atmosphere is what compels others to want to be in your company. The climate in your home, in your relationship not only affects you but it affects your loved ones and those who come in contact with you. A pleasant climate in relationship is what makes your wife or your husband anticipate coming home. The same goes for an unpleasant, foul climate. It cause everyone to scatter. No one wishes to be in your company or have you around. Others wish that you would hurry up and leave. What a lonesome life that would be.

Anyone in your environment can feel the effects of your atmosphere. It is amazing how a newborn can feel the atmosphere. Joyful, happy children are as they are because the consistancy of a pleasant atmosphere. Cranky, crying, fussy babies are sometimes like they are because of a consistent, unpleasant atmosphere. Sometimes people are often sickly because of unpleasant, foul atmospheres.

The reason your spouse hates coming home is because the climate at home is filled with tension. No one wishes to live in a trash can with all kinds of filth. It does not matter if that is where you came from. You're an adult now. You can change and positively charge your atmosphere. You can positively control your climate, your environment, and your atmosphere. How? By changing your thinking. Think optimistically. The Bible tells us (Phil. 4:8) to, "Think on things that are lovely, think on things that are pure, think on things that are of a good report, if there be any virture or commendable quality in you, think on these things." Why? Because God knew there are times and many reasons we could think on hateful things, we could have impure thoughts and "Out of the abundance of the heart the mouth speaks." There are many opportunites to think about the bad report, but He says, "If there be any goodness in you, think on these things." You can change your atmosphere by speaking positively. Life has enough challenges for one to overcome without you adding to the challenge. Maintaining a pleasant atmosphere is a daily effort. It can be done. It starts with you. I challenge you to start today. If you are an optimistic person, maintain your stance and watch your climate change for the good.

18

Hold That Thought

Did you know you can control your thoughts? As small an instrument it is that holds our thoughts as it compares to the rest of our body, it governs our whole body. It governs our actions and reactions. It plays a big part in our perception of life and all it has to offer. The Bible admonishes us to keep our thoughts under control. Do not allow your thoughts or your mind to run tangently. In relationship there is a mood, an attitude that sets the mood and temperature of your relationship. Each day you wake up and through out the day you determine the mood of your relationship. You can say the right thing and it will set an atmosphere, a mood that will create a pleasant memory. Anytime you wish to create a romantic mood for the evening, it first started in your mind. You made a conscious effort to set your mind, your thoughts on things that will create a romantic evening and when you did it, it worked. When you make up in your mind you are going to change the climate in your relationship for the better, it first starts in your mind.

First the mind, and the rest will follow. In order to have a better, closer, and loving relationship you must make up your mind. Set it and become persistant to the task. It may take time but the end results are so rewarding. You will wonder why didn't you do this a long time ago. Please know when you decide to do this, just as it is an adjustment on your part, it will be a change and adjustment on your mate's part as well. It may throw them for a loop for a minute but as you persist in your endeavor to have a better relationship, it will work out for the good of both parties involved. When someone is constantly angry, fussy, and negative it only goes back to 'what is on your mind?' It reflects back to what have you been thinking about. The next time you feel uptight and angry, before you lash out and cause irreversible damage, think about what's been on your mind. Are you a negative thinker? Do you look at everything in life from a pessimistic view? What does your peers, your loved ones think of you? Do they view you as a menace to society? Not because they want to but because that is what you give off.

The Bible references the mind many times and how we are to, "Let this mind be in you which was in Christ Jesus." Even when we were deliberately doing wrong in God's eyesight, He still loved us and even though He's an all knowing God and knows the future, He knew about us before we knew ourselves, yet He died for us. He sees and knows the good potential in us when we do not see it in ourselves. We should have this mindset. We should see the good in life, in others even when visibly we cannot see it. That is why getting to know the heart of a person is so important. Do not allow your negative actions to overshadow the goodness of your heart because then it becomes difficult and sometimes extremely challenging for others especially those close to you to see there is a good, fun, loving, caring person in you. You know it's there but no one else knows it's there. People will not know the real you and will have a distorted outlook of who you are. When you come around, you clear out the room as though you have some contagious disease. You will sit lonesomely in a room watching others have a great time without you. Others will love to see you leave.

What do you say to yourself? If you think you are a failure, guess what? You will act like a failure, you will talk like a failure, and you will respond like a failure. However, if you think you are a winner, you will be a winner, you will think like a winner, you will talk like a winner, you will respond like a winner, and you will have the mindset of a winner. A winner puts his best foot forward. A winner never quits doing his best. A winner speaks nothing but positive words to himself and to others. That is how God sees you, as a winner. If He sees that in you despite your pitfalls, then I think you should join Him and view yourself as a winner. That is why the Bible is a great manual to live by. In this world we live in, we must constantly feed our minds with positive words. A fruitful mind is a terrible thing to waste. Why be unfruitful when you can be fruitful? What you feed your mind will become your dialog and your dialog will become your deeds which will form a perception of who you are.

The Bible makes the statement, "Sheep beget sheep". The same goes for optimistic, positive, energetic, fun, and loving people. They beget of their kind. Fruitful people beget and attract fruitful people. Unfruitful beget and attract the unfruitful. Misery loves company. It is a choice. If you want others to be around you, if you want others to cherish your company, you must make yourself enjoyable to be around. If you want your loved ones to be able to approach you and seek your advice, make yourself approachable.

That is the one thing that make others seek advice from you is you are approachable and easy to talk to. You make others FEEL like they can trust your expertise in a situation.

The saying, "Junk in, junk out", is one I'd like to replace with, "Good things in, good things out." To the pure all things are pure. To the ugly, all things are ugly. Everybody is not out to do you harm. There are those who desire to do you good, but how do you view yourself? What goes on in your thought life concerning 'you?' Do you feel you deserve the good things life has to offer? How do you view yourself?

When someone offers to do and say something nice to you, do you say the opposite? Do you shrub it off? Or do you embrace it? If it is true about you, you should embrace it. Did you know you train people how to treat you. If you're always negative and unaccepting of great compliments from others, next time they may not say or do anything good for you because you say and show you do not accept it. It all begans in the mind. Learn to accept the good things life has to offer. Be approachable. Make up in your mind to exemplify the winner that you are. You will find others will love to be around you. You will notice your attitude will change concerning yourself. You will began to become upbeat mentally, physically, and emotionally. Make a change for the better today. It all starts in your mind then in your dialog and consequently in your   deeds.

19

Affirm and Confirm

In relationships, it is necessary to affirm and confirm. Never assume your loved ones know how you feel. You say, "I tell them all the time." Sometimes when life deals you a low blow or you are feeling a little down and out, it is good to be reminded that you are loved and you are important. Emotions are always churning, whether or not there is a response or not does not dispell the activity of emotions, particularly in women. As we stated earlier, women are emotional. That is the way God made us. Just think, if women were not emotional we would be a cold, heartless people. Emotions are a good thing. Emotions keep women in touch with the warm side of life. It helps us familiarize ourselves with reality. If women did not have emotions, we would be hard, resentful, and vengeful. Please do not misunderstand my saying this as a throw off to our counterparts.

Because men are not emotional is a wonderful thing for a woman. It is a stabilizing factor for women. It helps us not get so far out in left field. At the same time, emotions for women are good for men when handled correctly. Men are not driven by emotion but are driven by ego. They are strong, hard, robust, and performance driven. That is the way God made them. It does a man good to hear compliments and praise for his performance. Just think if men were emotional? We would both be crying all the time. There would be a lack of strength when one is weak. We would both have a bad day. We would both be down in the dumps. It would be like the blind leading the blind and we both fall in the ditch together with no one to get us out. Thank God for strong men however, a woman's emotions are good for her man to keep him in touch with reality as well and to help soften the blow sometimes. If women were made up like men, we would be hunters, hard, strong, robust and our men would be clueless to the softer side of life. That is what makes us both unique in our own way. Thank God we are different. God made us to compliment each other. One attributes and helps the other. That is what makes us whole.

It is a wonderful thing to allow your mate to become who they are and you become who you are and the both of you pick up where the other leaves off. That is the art of making your very own relational rhythm. Instead of pointing out your differences, compliment them, embrace them, and work it for the good of both. That is how you make it work. You fall in love, you marry because you realize your life is so much better with this person. After you marry, you discover your individuality and how you differ from each other. You began to create your rhythm. You compliment your differences and pick up where the other leaves off. You start putting the puzzle pieces together that makes your relationship work. You settle in and enjoy your special bond and what you have because you realized you really do have something special. Learn to have fun. Ceate memories and do things that years from now you will cherish between the two of you. By then you are understanding one another's heart, walking together, and relishing your union. God intended for marriage to be fun, loving, God - based (because He instituted and manufactured it), full of intrigue and spontaneity, and exciting. If your marriage is not what I've just described then you must decide to make it that way. If it's boring, dull, cold, unloving, full of tension, and stress, you know who instigated this behavior? The devil, and he works through people but that can change today. Make up in your mind to make your relationship fun and beating on a very positive rhythmic note.

Donna Ritchie

20

Understanding Your Woman

Understanding is crucial in relationships. Knowing the heart of a person is also imperative. When you understand where a person's heart is, you really understand them to the point where if they are having a bad day, you will know it's not you, it is because they are having a bad day. In order to understand a woman you must communicate with her. Find out what makes her tick and what makes her not tick. Find out what she likes and what she dislikes. Understand and know her mood changes. Know that women handle life through their emotions. Everything she does is derived through her emotions; the way she dresses, her thoughts, her hairstyle, even down to the way she dresses her children. For example if you, the husband, tells her she would look really classy in that black dress, though she agrees with you, often times if her emotions tells her, "Well, the brown dress will look better". Guess who typically wins? Her emotions; the brown dress. However, you should still compliment her because she really does want to look her best for you and if she feels better in that brown dress, that is the one she will most likely wear.

The Bible admonishes us to be patient, quick to hear, and slow to speak. You will be amazed at how this will enhance your relationship with her. Studies show that women have more dialog than men. It is helpful to listen and respond in a positive way, always encouraging, and lifting her up.

No matter how long you've been married, you want to continue being a gentleman and treating your wife with the highest respect. Never take her or what she does for granted. Be reminded of your dating days and the things you did during that time. Maintain your best behavior as you did dating. Opening the car door, making her feel like she's the only one for you, is key in relationship. You do not mistreat her and treat everyone else better than you treat her. Always compliment your wife. You do not embarrass her because she will patiently get even with you. She is a multiplier. She multiplies what is given to her. When she is assured that she is truly loved and top priority in your life, it is easy for her to submit to you. She will go through great lengths to make you happy. A woman embraces the element of surprise. Unexpected surprises are sure winners. Your gentle touch means positively more than what you can fathom. A kind word in the midst of chaos goes a long way with her. Think of how girls cleave to their fathers. They feel protected, secure, and loved by their fathers. This is what most woman are accustomed to from childhood. Little girls love to be held and cuddled by their fathers and that is what women desire from their husband. It is important that your woman feel that sense of security, comfort, and love. Often times what your woman may be angry about has nothing to do with what she is angry about. It is simply the lack of your affection and attention to her. I encourage you to spend time with her. Be consistent in showing your love for her. Don't assume she knows you love her but tell her and show her you love her everyday. Now that you know she needs to hear, "I Love You" everyday, why not start today? Love is an action. Love says and exemplifies lovely behavior.

Donna Ritchie

21

Understanding Your Man

Men are obviously different than women. They are different physically, mentally, genetically, and in all facets of life. It is beneficial to understand their language. Since we know they are performance driven, women must pay attention to what they do. For example, if your husband is the repairman in your home, be thankful you do not have to pay a repairman to fix your repairs. If your husband sends you occasional roses or encourages you to go have a good time while he watches the children, he is saying, "I Love You." He is saying, "I love you enough to freely give you some personal time to take a break from your routine. Let me watch the children and you take care of you." He is saying, "I recognize what you do on a daily basis and I want you to take a break and relax. Take care of yourself."

That kind of behavior speaks volumes. As his wife, you should take him up on his offer wholeheartidly. If you do not, shame on you. Do not get angry, frustrated, or upset.

What I am saying is, get to know your husband. Understand his language, both verbal and non-verbal. Understand, sometimes when he comes home and passes out asleep on the sofa it is probably because he is truly tired and because he knows how his day went all day. He needs to know there will be peace when he awakes. This is not an excuse for those who are clueless and refuse information as to what it takes being a husband to his wife, understanding, and considering what it takes to be his wife and mother in the family. There is a role everyone has to adhere to. Yes, everyone gets tired and would love a Calgon moment but reality still goes on. However, with balance there comes a time when everything and everyone must be placed on hold and you must take a 'time out' for you and for each other. This is a somber statement however, think about it. When you die you will want to be remembered for the things you did together, not how clean you always kept the house, or how well you kept the car clean. These examples are very important in life but the strongest memory you will want your loved ones to have is the good times you had together, the walks in the park, those fun things you did togther, and the private, sweet conversations you shared. That is what makes the thought of you become so overwhelming. That is how you want to be remembered in life and when you are laid to rest.

22

Listen With Your Heart

In order to know someone you must spend time with them. You must communicate with them. When there is a miscommunication in a relationship between a man and a woman, there is a misunderstanding of some sort. When a disagreement occurs, sometimes it is derived from an assumption. I have come to the conclusion, women are like computers. You can never understand them. Why? Because often times women cannot understand themselves. It is not a bad thing or an excuse, it is the way it is at times. However, women must fight hard to keep an even keel emotionally so others will not perceive them to be schizophrenic. On the other hand, there are some men who are walking volcanos, full of rage, and anger or those with a pessimistic nature that needs to be abolished. When you exemplify inconsistant behavior it becomes difficult for others to befriend you. You never know how to take a person who is inconsistent in their behavior. With the constant help of the supernatural power (God), self discipline, and control this behvior can be subdued.

It is highly imperative that couples learn to listen to what each is saying. Your spouse would rather talk to you than someone else. Who better for them to communicate with...than you?

You will be astounded and amazed at how down to earth God is when you ask Him to help you be the best husband or wife to your mate. He will give you great innovative ideas to enhance your relationship. He will open your understanding to situations. He will guide you in your endeavor to becoming a great husband or wife to your mate. And as long as you deal with your inconsistancies in life, He will sometimes hide that from your mate as well. He cares a great deal about you and your mate.

The Bible (Col. 3:1-3) talks about our lives being hid in Christ and you know what that means? When Christ is living in your life and you are allowing Him to dwell in your heart, He will not only guide you into ALL truth but He will hide those areas in your life that are not like Him until you (with effort) get it right, which just stopped all excuses for not behaving correctly.

A man should diligently seek out ways to understand his wife and the wife should do the same for her husband. Why? Because neither has never been the other. In reality there is always something going on emotionally in women. Women are so full of emotion and there are so many hormonal changes that it sometimes confuses her. It does not negate the fact we are fearfully and wonderfully made by God. However, there is a constant emotional roller coaster ride and some of it is due to hormonal balances or imbalances. Some of it is due to medicine and its side effects. There is a constant emotional challenge which must be dealt with. The challenge is whether we adhere to the good hormonal days where we strut ourselves like 'we are woman,' 'we are loved', or whether we adhere to the urge to turn into Cat Woman. Women go through PMS, having babies, not having babies and desiring one, and menopause better known as the mid life crisis because emotionally it sometimes feel like they are in a crisis. This is not an excuse to adhere to the crisis. We must resist the temptation to turn into Cat Woman. On the other hand, the poor men are scratching their heads trying to figure out and understand why women are so emotional.

Has it ever dawned on you the reason your man is left in la- la land when it comes to the intricate details of you as woman? Your man desires to love you and provide for you but it is very difficult to do so if all he gets is complaints, gripes, and attitudes that defiles the room and stinks up the atmosphere in your relationship. Help your man understand you. He's never been a woman. He is clueless as to what goes on in a woman's body, mind, and emotions and rightfully so because he is a man. He does not know what it's like to have PMS. He thought PMS stood for '**P**retty **M**ean **S**istah' because he sees this beast appear once a month more or less at times. Sit down with your man and inform him of what takes place in your body, mind, and emotions. Sit down and talk. Communicate because he really does not know what it is like to be you. He doesn't know what you have to deal with on a daily basis. I believe when he knows what you have to go through on a daily basis then he will be able to cope with it with great understanding. If he looks confused at the onset of your conversation it is probably because he is confused. This is not a put down to men nor women because sometimes a woman does not know what is going on in her body and is trying to figure it out herself. Please understand some things are the way they are because that is just the way they are. Some things are included in life's journey but how we deal with it determines the outcome.

Please understand women must resist the urge to let the Cat Woman out of the bag. Keep sister girl under restraints. She's ugly and deviously dangerous. She plays revenge at the drop of a hat. To say, "I cannot help it", is not acceptable. That is not how you became involved in this relationship. When you were dating, you kept her under tight control. Why let her out now? Information and understanding is everything. I think that is why some men walk out of relationships because they are tired of trying to figure women out. They are tired of the struggle and the fight. They want peace and less complication to life. Generally men are advocates for keeping things simple (KISS: **K**eep **I**t **S**imple **S**weety).

Women must aspire to be consistantly even and balanced emotionally. Problems occur when we adhere to the imbalances in our lives. It is either women are too far in left field or they are too far in right field. There must be a consistent balance emotionally and when there is not, talk about it. Prewarn and resist the tempation. Often times it is best to find a quiet place and collect yourself. Dust yourself off and come out with a better version of yourself.

A man needs to know he is secure in the relationship. He needs to know his business is not spread abroad. When he is weak, he needs assurance from you that he has a shoulder to lean on and still be the man. He needs someone to be there with a kind, understanding, and loving ear. Sometimes he needs cuddling. Think about a little boy and how he cleaves to his mother. Little boys really love their mothers, why? Because they know Mom will take care of them. Mom looks out for her boys. She expresses her confidence in him. She praises him for what he does. He will stick his chest out like Tarzan for his mother's compliments and accolates. When you look at your man, see that little boy inside. He grew up with praise. He is used to the notion that someone is in his corner rooting for him. He is used to being called, "The Man."

Because you are married does not lend you the right to lose integrity, dignity, or self control. Remember, doing something good and right on a consistent basis goes much deeper than the deed itself. It creates those things money cannot buy. It creates trust, respect, and a thriving, exciting relationship.

Donna Ritchie

23

What does "I Love You" mean?

'I Love You' are three words often misunderstood by the masses. It is said many ways and interpreted in many ways as well. Men say, "I Love You", differently than women. Men say, "I Love You", not only in word but in deed. When a man provides for his family, places a roof over their head, and takes care of his family, he is saying, "I Love You." That is why it is a huge blow to him when his efforts of provision are slighted or regarded as nothing. When a man leaves his home to face the rough terrain out there in the world, it is important for him to know he's appreciated for what he does for his family. It is crucial when he comes home there is peace and rest for him. A good man provides for his family and works hard to make them happy. This is not a derrogative comment however, because many are unaware of what he has to encounter throughout the day, it is so good for him to know that his house is a home at the end of his day. Think of single parenting and what it takes to provide for you and your children.

When you are married, there are times your husband endures the stress that goes along with obtaining and maintaining a steady income for his family. He toils with the notion of, "What if I lose my job? How will I take care of my family?" Most men are driven to make money and be the provider for their family. It is a part of their make up as a man. If he cannot do so, it makes him feel like he is less than a man.

When your husband goes beyond providing for you and does little extra things outside of the general duties he does for his family because he is performance driven, he is saying, "I Love You", through his performance, not necessarily in word. When he does it, learn to recognize it and thank him for it. Do not ever take him or his kindness for granted. Celebrate him for what he does for you and the children. Pay attention to what he does for you. Remember men are not as verbal as women. They are performers; they are doers. Catch on to what your man is doing, both verbally and non verbally. You will be astounded at how much he really loves you and how often he says it in deed. Focus in on the good things he does. I guarantee you, as you praise him for what he does, he will like doing it and he will most likely want to do more for you. Whether he does more or not, thank him for what he does.

Women say, "I Love You", differently than men. When your wife takes care of your business, the children, and sometimes your immediate family, she is saying, "I Love You." When she prepares your meal, keeps your clothes clean, takes care of your home, and takes care of the children, she is saying, "I Love You", enough to maintain the homefront while you are away. Because she cleans, cooks, and does what she does and is great at it, does not mean she loves what she does. So acknowledging what she does, appreciating her for it, and helping her makes her feel like you love her enough to take to heart what she does. Have you noticed the both of you are working as a team? She is noticing you and you are noticing her and how you love one another. You are complimenting each other. You are picking up where the other has left off.

If both of you are working it is important to help each other maintain the home and children together. When a woman comes home and has to take care of the children, the homework, the cat, the dog, and the housework, she is too tired to take care of anything else. She hasn't had time to even take care of herself, not to mention taking care of her husband. This is why she is irritable because there is no rest in the Inn for her. She is mentally and physcially exhausted. She needs your help. She would love to come home and relax with a hot meal awaiting her after working all day. Her mind and body does not rest until her children are fed and in bed, the house is cleaned, and all is at rest. It is imperative that you help one another so everyone can rest together. Then she can have time for herself and spend time with her man.

When a woman takes off her work hat and switch to her mommy hat, that in and of itself is an awesome task. To take that for granted is an absolute no-no. Thank her for what she does. Appreciate her for her efforts and endeavors. Helping her says, "Thank you", in a big way. Women, if your man helps you, thank him and do not shoot him down if it is not done exactly like you would do it. He is trying to make things better. Give him credit for trying. This all goes back to each being patient with the other while gaining knowledge and understanding. This is what makes relationships work. It promotes courtesy, respect, teamwork, and affirmation in a relationship.

It is important for you, the husband, to pay attention to the way she says, "I Love You." The one thing that melted my butter when I first got married til this day is my husband telling me, "You do not have to do anything you do not want to", (i.e. cook, housework, etc) and guess what? I do it with joy and not grief. I don't care to cook but I will do it to the best of my ability because I love my husband. Oh by the way, I can cook (smile). It is something about when you tell a person they don't have to do a thing, it makes them want to do it all the more. Here again, he knew my heart. He knows I will do what it takes to make things work.

As the two of you begin to walk and work in harmony and not pull against each other, things change for the better. You change a stressful atmosphere into a pleasant, positive one. You will do.... because you want to, not because you are forced to do it. It makes life so much easier to live. It makes living with and loving your mate so much fun and so interesting. Ladies in particular have to take a break. Sometimes dotting the 'i' and crossing the 't' can wait. Your loved ones would like to remember you as being fun to be around, refreshing, and not a housewife fanatic. Ladies and gentlemen, great memories are created by those fun, loving things done with one another. You only have one life to live. Why not enjoy it to the fullest with the one you love? Don't take life so serious. Don't become so tight that you squeeze the life out of your relationship. Have fun and become spontaneous with your spouse, with your children. They will treasure those moments with you. You will experience fun and fulfilment like you have never felt before and you will find yourself looking forward to the next time of suspense. This is what living life is all about.

Make yours and your loved ones lives enriched. It is in you. You may have to practice and learn, but start now. Life will become so rewarding for you and your family.

Donna Ritchie

24

Presentation is Everything

Your presentation is everything. Hygiene is so important when you are in relationship. People like to see and smell great things. When I think of something that looks breath taking I think of a rose. It not only looks beautiful but it smells beautiful and fresh. Good hygiene is a turn on in relationship. When you were dating you wanted to impress the one you were interested in. You not only wanted to look good but smell good. Putting your best forward does not stop after you get married. Keep your best foot forward because that is what helped you get the man or woman of your dreams and it will be the thing that keeps your relationship romantic, interesting, entrigueing and full of life. Find out what your mate likes and aim to please. Keep in mind presentation is key.

As I stated earlier in the book, refer back to your boyfriend/girlfriend days and the things done to impress. The atmosphere, the climate, the words used, the tone, the body language, and the great lengths gone through to satisfy the other does not have to cease after the 'I do's are done.

Marriage is what you make it. You can choose to make it exciting and full of suspense. Go against the grain and determine to make your relationship work. It takes two teamplayers to do this. Go against the grain and see how less you can argue. Aspire to get alone most of the time. Maintain the romance and the element of suspense by cherishing and enjoying one another. Take care of each other and do not be afraid to express the love and concern in your relationship.

When there are children involved you not only owe it to yourselves and your relationship to spend quality time together, but you owe it to them for their foundational security. Do not allow life's demands to inhale the life out of your relationship. Have fun together; be polite to one another. Acknowledge, consider, confirm, and affirm one another and cherish the love you share. It makes you feel good when you are cleaned up and looking nice. I am encouraging you to look nice, smell good, and take care of yourself for you first, and then for your mate.

25

Passions of the Heart

Comprised in the sanctity of marriage is the notion that marriage renders one vulnerable to the other and vice versa. A marriage ceremony consists of two people committing to life- long vows before the Almighty God and to each other however, it is also trusting someone with your heart; trusting someone to enter into the inner most part of you. Therefore you must proceed with extreme caution. It does not matter how long you have been married, proceeding with caution is crucial. Proceed with caution by what you say, how you say it, what you do, and how you do it. Am I saying walk on eggshells for the rest of your life? No. I am saying you must be careful and mindful of how you handle the other. Can you do this if there is a disagreement? Yes, you can. It is described as keeping the baby while throwing out the bath water. You only throw out the water if it is really necessary. Sometimes you can keep both and spare the harsh feelings. It takes a wise man or woman to deal with a situation while maintaining your cool and still get the best results for the two of you.

One thing about a good marriage is having two people who know who they are individually; two people who are confident they possess greatness inside and work together to bring that goodness out of the other. I believe every marital relationship has the potential to do this despite your past. It is a determined decision one must make in order to achieve a good, wholesome relationship.

We all dream of that perfect relationship where Mr. Right comes in on a white horse to whisk his damsel away. You can have Mr. Right or Mrs. Right by showing unconditional love, patience, and teamwork. It is so gratifying to know you have someone cheering for you in your corner. It is important to express, "Yes, I am in your corner."

It is important to express the good things about your mate on a consistent basis. I have a news flash for you. Absolutely no one is a detailed, 'down to the tee' mind reader. If you don't say it or show it to the point where the other understands completely what you are doing, the other will not know or will not have gotten your message.

If you want Mrs. Right to enter your room, turn on the charm and act like Mr. Right. If you want Mr. Right to come knocking on your door, turn on the charm and act like Mrs. Right. Words, body language, and what you do are all welcomed and play an intricate part in setting the tone. Men, if your wife loves to see you dressed like Tarzan, then start beating on your chest and yelling, "Roar!" She's your woman. She is the only one who matters. Getting the point to her that it's all about 'you,' "I Love you," and "I am out to make 'you' happy", is extremely imperative.

Girlfriend, if your husband is turned on by you looking sexy with his favorite perfume, even though you have children, put those children to bed or send them to grandma's, take your vitamins early, and bring out Mrs. Hot Mama and steam up the room. There is nothing wrong with that. Do not be ashamed. Your aim ought to be that you make it hard for anyone to come in on your turf. You should make your relationship so passionately interesting that the ecstasy of suspense is at its peak all of the time. This is how God imagined marriage to be.

God created marriage to be fun. That is why His words admonishes us to do good to others. Others mean anyone other than yourself, which includes your spouse. He tells us to get an understanding because when you understand a thing or in this case, when you understand someone, often times you can handle matters better because you know where it is coming from.

There was a story of a Christian man involved in pornography that felt it was wrong and who did not want to be involved in it. He reluctantly told his wife and to his amazement instead of her going off on him and telling him how wrong he was, she decided to comfort him and help him get through it by trying to understand where it was coming from; by understanding why was he involved in it. Because he was already guilty, it was obvious he knew it was wrong. She proceeded to help correct the situation and would lovingly check on him throughout the day to see if he was okay. I love the fact she stated to him, "We will get through this together."

That is what marriage is all about. There were no finger pointing and fault finding that was already done without assistance from anyone else. The thought dawned on her that either he had a past altercation or there was an enormous problem he was dealing with. Notice, she did not condone his behavior because it is Biblically wrong to be involved in pornography however, she took a less hostile approach and still obtained the right results. It takes a real woman with much wisdom and strength to do that. She knew he was not cheating on her. This is an example of trust roots going much deeper than the notion. When you can walk through the muddy streams of life with someone whose actions do not deserve a kind word or a patient hand of comfort in the time of crisis but gets it anyway, that is trusts roots growing deeper and stronger. Being there for each other, helping one another, and committing to one another is the glue that keeps marriages long and lasting.

Starting today, commit to increasing and emphasizing the greatness in your mate and decrease to the point of no return the negative aspects of your mate, of your relationship and yes, decrease highlighting your faults about yourself to others. In other words, don't live a life of personal denial, but deal with it. Get through it and confess the good things about you, about your relationship, and about your mate.

Turn on the charm; keep the passion, spontaneity, ecstasy, romance, and excitement in your relationship. Celebrate your mate, your relationship. Life is too short for stress, worry, and arguing.

You've heard the saying, "You win more flies with honey, than with vinegar", which is true. Start winning with kind words, loving behavior, teamwork, understanding each other, and focusing on the others' happiness (*while not being difficult to make happy*).

What you don't know, 'ask' and/or read articles and books on men and/or women. Associate with winning couples, people who are going in a positive direction in life. Then you too will be on your way to creating your own rhythm in your maximized relationship.

Donna Ritchie

26

Conclusion

It is my focus to enlighten you with the knowledge that you can "Maximize Your Relationship" and that there is a rhythm to it all. You can have a lifelong, loving relationship.

Please understand when two people commit to each other, it is a known fact that there will be occasions of disagreements. It is because you have two individuals becoming one, that is what makes life interesting for the two of you. However, it does not mean you have to become two disagreeable people. You can maintain your togetherness despite disagreeing. Allow room for individuality because living with a robot is cold, hardening, lifeless, and no fun. Disagreeing is a bump in the road and should be the exception and not the rule. See how less you can disagree and focus on how much fun you can create. Loosen up and don't take life so seriously. You only have one life, you might as well enjoy it with the one you love. Be careful with your words and choose them wisely because they are those things that cannot be reversed. Speak positive words over your spouse and your relationship.

Be proud of your relationship. Don't be ashamed to express your affection. Crank up the heat of ecstasy and passion. It does great wonders for your relationship. Make time for being together. "Therefore what God hath joined together let no man put asunder." Do not allow excuses, circumstance, or people to inhale the life and vitality out of your lives together. Earnestly pursue creative ways to enhance and make better your relationship.

There are many fun, exciting, inexpensive, and thoughtful ways to keep the spontaneity in your relationship. For example, you can have a picnic in your own house, just the two of you. You can have a home cooked meal by candlelight. You can go for a ride in the country and cozy up in the car. You can go to the park and let the kids run around while you spend time together. You can go to a movie and have popcorn together. There are countless ways to keep the suspense and fun in your relationship. Marriage is God's gift to you, what you do with it, is your gift to Him. He meant for it to be fun and exciting. Since it is what you make of it, make it fun and fulfilling for the both of you. Maximize your God given time together.

In my next book, we will dig deeper into the complexities of 'two becoming one' and dispel the myths in relationships and focus on the creative ways to maintain a healthy relationship.

For additional copies of this book, please visit my website below. Thank you for your purchase and support.

Donna Ritchie

Website: www.donnaritchie.com

Notes